FUNDAMENTALS OF APPLIED PHYSICS–II (PART-I)

VIBRATION -SIMPLE HARMONIC MOTION, WAVE MOTION AND ITS APPLICATIONS, RAY OPTICS AND ITS APPLICATIONS, ELECTROSTATICS

GOPAL CHAKRABORTY

Copyright © GOPAL CHAKRABORTY
All Rights Reserved.

This book has been self-published with all reasonable efforts taken to make the material error-free by the author. No part of this book shall be used, reproduced in any manner whatsoever without written permission from the author, except in the case of brief quotations embodied in critical articles and reviews.

The Author of this book is solely responsible and liable for its content including but not limited to the views, representations, descriptions, statements, information, opinions and references ["Content"]. The Content of this book shall not constitute or be construed or deemed to reflect the opinion or expression of the Publisher or Editor. Neither the Publisher nor Editor endorse or approve the Content of this book or guarantee the reliability, accuracy or completeness of the Content published herein and do not make any representations or warranties of any kind, express or implied, including but not limited to the implied warranties of merchantability, fitness for a particular purpose. The Publisher and Editor shall not be liable whatsoever for any errors, omissions, whether such errors or omissions result from negligence, accident, or any other cause or claims for loss or damages of any kind, including without limitation, indirect or consequential loss or damage arising out of use, inability to use, or about the reliability, accuracy or sufficiency of the information contained in this book.

Made with ♥ on the Notion Press Platform
www.notionpress.com

Dedicated

to

The memory of my beloved father

Late Sankar Chakraborty

Whose honesty and devotion to education is ever rememberable

"The highest education is that which does not merely give us information but that makes our life in harmony with all existence."~~
Rabindranath Tagore

Contents

Foreword

This book on "Fundamentals of Applied Physics (Part-I)" contains the chapter like **Vibration -Simple Harmonic Motion, Wave motion and its applications, Ray Optics and its applications, Electrostatics** as per new syllabus introduced by West Bengal State Council of Technical and Vocational Education and Skill Development for the 2nd Semester Students of Diploma Engineering (Polytechnic).

This book is written in view of addition and alteration of Chapters and exercises have been done for the benefits of students, I hope this first edition will be well accepted by my respected teachers and my beloved students.

Preface

This book on "Fundamentals of Applied Physics (Part-I)" has been written with a view to cater the need of undergraduate Engineering students. This newly edition of book is written strictly in accordance with the new syllabus introduced by West Bengal State Council of Technical and Vocational Education and Skill Development for the 2nd Semester Students of Diploma Engineering (Polytechnic).

The book has been written in very lucid and simple English. While presenting the subject matter, it has been my constant conscious effort to give more depth of treatment and emphasis on the fundamentals. In doing so, I have deliberately avoided the unnecessary experimental complications on the one hand and undue mathematical treatment on the other. To illustrate the applications of the basic principles of the concept developed, in more or less simple form, numerous problems and multiple choice type questions have been appended towards the end of each Module.

I hope, this publication will also be response equally well by respected teachers and my beloved students of this book. Any suggestions, comments and constructive criticism of this first edition of this book are cordially invited and thank fully acknowledged both from students and teachers for further improvement of this book.

WBSCTVESD Curriculum for Diploma Courses in Engineering and Technology Semester-II (Theory), Applied Physics –II

Course Code: BS104

Course Title: Applied Physics –II

Number of Credits: 3 (L: 2, T: 1, P: 0)

Prerequisites: High School Level Physics

Course- Category: BS

Course Objectives

Applied Physics aims to give an understanding of this world both by observation and by prediction of the way in which objects behave. Concrete use of physical principles and analysis in various fields of engineering and technology are given prominence in the course content. The course will help the diploma engineers to apply the basic concepts and principles to solve broad- based engineering problems and to understand different technology based applications.

Course Content

Unit -1: Wave motion and its applications

Simple Harmonic Motion (SHM): definition, expression for displacement, velocity, acceleration, time period, frequency etc. study of vibrations of cantilever and determination of its time period, Free, damped and forced vibrations with examples.

Wave motion, transverse and longitudinal waves with examples (Sound and light waves) definitions of wave velocity, frequency and wave length and their relationship, equation of a plane progressive wave. Principle of superposition of waves and beat formation.

Acoustics of buildings- reverberation, reverberation time, methods to control reverberation time , noise, coefficient of absorption of sound, Ultrasonic waves – Introduction and properties, engineering and medical applications of ultrasonic.

Unit – 2: Optics

Basic optical laws: reflection and refraction, refractive index, Images and image formation by thin lenses, lens & lens maker's formula, (no deduction) power of lens, magnification simple numerical problems.

Total internal reflection, Critical angle and conditions for total internal reflection, applications of total internal reflection in optical fiber.

Optical Instruments; simple and compound microscope, astronomical telescope (refracting, Ray Diagram and formula for magnification). Interference and diffraction of light (Qualitative ideas only).

Unit – 3: Electrostatics

Coulombs law, unit of charge, Electric field, Electric lines of force and their properties, Electric flux,

Electric potential and potential difference, Gauss law (statement only) Application of Gauss law to find electric field due to a charged sphere.

Capacitor and its working, types of capacitors, Capacitance and its units. Capacitance of a parallel plate capacitor (formula only), Series and parallel combination of capacitors formula (related numerical problems), dielectric and its effect on capacitance, dielectric break down.

Unit – 4: Current Electricity

Electric Current and its units, Direct and alternating current, resistance and its units, Specific resistance, Conductance, Specific conductance, Series and parallel combination of resistances. Factors affecting resistance of a wire, carbon resistance and colour coding.

Ohm's law, Kirchhoff's laws, Wheatstone bridge, Carrey Foster Bridge and its applications, Concept of terminal potential difference and Electro motive force (EMF).

Heating effect of current, electric power, electric energy and its units (related numerical problems)

Thermoelectric effect: Seebeck &Peltier effects.

Unit -5: Electromagnetism

Magnetic field and its origin, units, Lorentz force (force on moving charge in magnetic field).Biot- Savart law, Application to Straight, Conductor & circular loop; concept of magnetic dipole. Force on current carrying conductor, Torque on rectangular coil placed magnetic field concept of electromagnetic induction, Faraday's Laws, Moving coil galvanometer; principle, construction and working, Conversion of a galvanometer into ammeter and voltmeter.

Types of magnetic materials; dia, para and ferromagnetic with their properties.

Unit-6: Semiconductor Physics

Energy bands in solids, Types of materials (insulator, semi-conductor, conductor), intrinsic and extrinsic semiconductors, p-n junction, junction diode and V-I characteristics, Diode as rectifier- half wave and full wave rectifier (Centre taped) & circuit symbol.

Transistor, Block diagram types (pnp and npn) & circuit symbol, transistor as an amplifier CE mode

(Circuit diagram and concept).

Photocells, Solar cells and LED working principle and engineering application.

Unit-7: Modern Physics

Bohr's atom model and concept energy levels, ionization and excitation potentials, X-rays, Production (Coolidge tube) continuous and characteristic-X-rays, soft and hard X-rays, and use,

Laser: spontaneous and stimulated emission; Laser light; He-Ne laser elementary characteristics, applications of lasers.

Fiber Optics: Introduction to optical fibers, mechanism of light propagation, applications.

Nanoscience and nanotechnology (Introduction only).

SEM-II (LAB), Applied Physics II Lab

Course Code: BS106

Course Tittle: Applied Physics II Lab

Number of Credits: 1 (L: 0, T: 0, P:2)

Prerequisites: NIL

Course Category: BS

Course Objectives:

Concrete use of physical principles and analysis in various fields of engineering and technology is very prominence. The course aims to supplement the factual knowledge gained in the lecture by first hand manipulation of apparatus. This will develop scientific temper and help to apply the basic concepts and principles in solving engineering and technology based problems. In addition, students get necessary confidence in handling equipment and thus learn various skills in measurement.

List of Practical/Activity: (To perform minimum 8 Practical)

1. To determine and verify the time period of oscillation of a cantilever.
2. To verify laws of refraction (Snell's law) using a glass slab.
3. To determine focal length and magnifying power of a convex lens by u-v method.
4. To verify Ohm's law by plotting graph between current and potential difference.

5. To verify laws of resistances in series by P.O. Box.

6. To verify laws of resistances in parallel by using Ammeter and Volt meter.

7. To verify Kirchhoff's law using electrical circuits.

8. To find resistance of a galvanometer by half deflection method.

9. To convert a galvanometer into an ammeter.

10. To convert a galvanometer into a voltmeter.

11. To verify inverse square law of radiations using a photo-electric cell.

12. To draw V-I characteristics of a semiconductor diode (Ge, Si) and determine its knee voltage.

13. To study the dependence of capacitance of a parallel plate capacitor on various factors and determine the permittivity of air at a place.

Overview of Chapters

CONTENTS

Chapter -3: Ray Optics and its applications

Chapter 4: Electrostatics

Chapter -1: Vibration -Simple Harmonic Motion

Chapter -1: Vibration -Simple Harmonic Motion

1.1 Introduction:

The movement of particles in rigid bodies may be in random fashion or along a definite path and sometimes in a repetitive manner. The motion of all moving bodies are of two types:

(a) The motion in which the body changes its position with respect to time and

(b) The motion in which the body moves to & fro about a fixed point. The first type of motion is called Translatory motion while the second one is called oscillatory or vibratory motion. The arc of a projectile, a flying aeroplane, a moving car etc are examples of translatory motion while the motion of a simple pendulum and vibration of stretched string are daily life examples of oscillatory motion. Recurring events take place in natural phenomena from the motion of electrons in atomic orbits to the appearance of Halley's Comet are every 75 years. An oscillatory motion that repeats itself in equal intervals of time is called periodic motion. The displacement of a particle executing periodic motion can be expressed in terms of sine or cosine functions and thus these motions are also called harmonic motion.

1.2 The causes of oscillation:

A body that undergoes periodic motion always has a stable equilibrium position, When it is moved away from this position and released, a force called restoring force or force of restitution, which is generally a function of displacement comes into play to pull it back towards equilibrium, But by the time the body moves to the equilibrium position it picks up some kinetic energy, overshoots, stops somewhere on the other side and is again pulled back towards equilibrium position. A ball rolling back and forth in a round bowl or a pendulum that swings back and forth past its straight-down position arc practical examples of periodic motion.

The restoring force can be expanded as powers of displacement x

Restoring force = $F(x) = a_0 + a_1 x^1 + a_2 x^2 + a_3 x^3 + \ldots\ldots$

Since there is no force on the particle when it is at rest, i.e. when x -0, F (%) = 0. Therefor $a_0 = 0$. For small displacements, the next term ($a_1 x$) is the most important. This term is linear in x. For restoring forces, a_1 is negative and the other co-efficient a_2 , a_3 etc. are increasingly smaller than a_1. Vibration in which the restoring force is directly proportional to the displacement is the simplest in nature and called simple-harmonic-motion (abbreviated SHM). A simple Harmonic Motion may be defined as a type of oscillatory or vibratory motion in which the force or acceleration of the particle is proportional to the displacement from its mean or equilibrium position and always directed towards the fixed mean position. Its importance lies in the fact that all vibrating systems execute SHM when the displacement is small and the periodic motion of any kind may be resolved into a number of SHMs.

A particle executing SHM is generally called a linear harmonic oscillator. The time required to complete one oscillation is called the time period (T). The number of oscillations made per second is called the frequency of the motion (v). The relation between time period and frequency is given by:

$T=1/v$ 1.1

The position at which no net force acts on an oscillatory body is called its equilibrium or mean position. The maximum displacement on either side of the equilibrium position is called the amplitude of the motion. The phase of a vibrating particle at any instant determines the state of displacement and motion of the particle at that instant. The initial phase of a vibrating body is called epoch.

1.3 Geometrical Interpretation of Simple Harmonic Motion:

The relationship between SHM and circular motion, can be understood with the help of figure 1.1. The figure is a graphical representation of phase- displacement curve of a SHM. The figure shows a circle of radius equal to a and a reference point P is moving with uniform angular velocity ω over the circumference of the circle, sweeping out an angle ωt which represents the phase of the SHM when P competes one revolution ωt changes from o to 2π. The distance of the foot of the perpendicular N drawn on AOB from different positions of P gives the corresponding displacement of the SHM. When the displacements and the corresponding phase angles are plotted along Y and X - axes respectively then the curve O'MOR is obtained, From Figure 1.1 we can write.

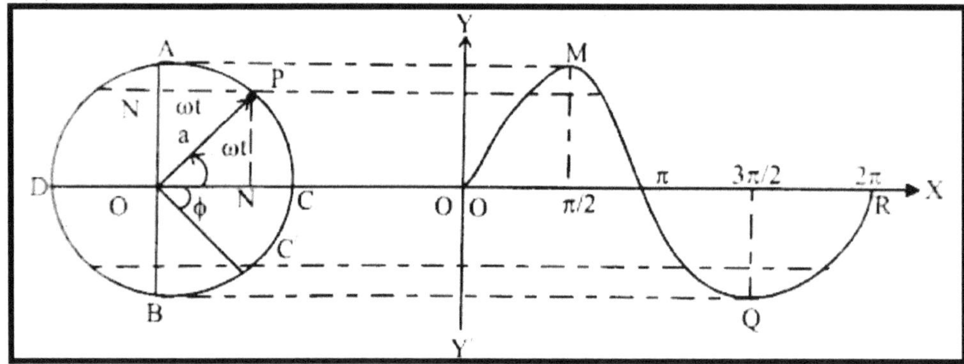

Figure 1.1: Phase displacement curve of SHM along with its reference circle

$PN/OP=y/a=Sinwt$

Or $y=aSinwt$ 1.2

Equation 1.2 represents the motion of the reference point P on the circumference of the circle. If the reference point starts moving from C' instead from C, then the phase angle will be: <C'OP = ωt + ϕ, where is the initial phase angle <C'OC called the epoch particle executing SHM. In that case, the motion of the reference point is represented by following equation:

$y=aSin(wt+\phi)$ 1.3

Since the co-ordinate axes x, and y are inter changeable, equation (1.3) can also be written any of the following form:

$x=aSin(wt+\phi)$

$x=aCos(wt+\phi)$

$y=aCos(wt+\phi)$ 1.4

1.4 Simple Harmonic Motion (SHM): Definition

A Simple Harmonic Motion, or SHM, is defined as a motion in which the restoring force is directly proportional to the displacement of the body from its mean position. The direction of this restoring force is always towards the mean position. Also, all simple harmonic motions are periodic in nature, but all periodic motions are not simple harmonic motions.

Characteristics of SHM:

(i) The motion is oscillatory and periodic ie, the motion is repeated after equal intervals of time;

(ii) The restoring force acting on the particle (or its acceleration) is always proportional to its displacement (measured along its path) from some fixed point on the path called its mean position.

(iii) The acceleration of the particle is always directed towards its mean position.

1.5 Differential Equation of Motion of SHM: Expression for displacement, velocity, acceleration, time period, frequency

Consider a particle of mass (m) executing Simple Harmonic Motion along a path x o x; the mean position at O. Let the speed of the particle be v0 when it is at position p (at a distance no from O).

At t = 0, the particle at P (moving towards the right), At t = t, the particle is at Q (at a distance x from O) with a velocity (v). The Restoring Force **F** at Q is given by

$$F \propto -x$$

$$F = -kx$$

$$m\frac{d^2x}{dt^2} = -kx$$

$$m\frac{d^2x}{dt^2} + kx = 0$$

$$\frac{d^2x}{dt^2} + \omega^2 x = 0$$

1.5

Equation 1.5 represent the differential equation of motion of a particle executing SHM. Where $\omega^2 = k/m$ is the natural angular frequency of oscillation and constant.

The differential equation for the Simple Harmonic Motion has the following solutions. Where x is the displacement of the particle executing SHM.

$x = a\,Sin(wt)$ 1.6

Differentiating this equation (1.6) for displacement with respect to time, The Velocity,

$$v = \frac{dx}{dt} = a\omega Cos\omega t$$

$$v = a\omega\sqrt{1 - Sin^2\omega t}$$

$$v = \omega\sqrt{a^2 - x^2}$$

$$v = \frac{2\pi}{T}\sqrt{a^2 - x^2}$$

1.7

Here T represented the Time period of oscillation.

Differentiating equation for the velocity given in (1.7) with respect to time, we obtain the Acceleration as

$$f = \frac{d^2x}{dt^2} = -a\omega^2 Sin\omega t$$

$$f = -\omega^2 x$$

$$f \propto -x$$

1.8

The equation (1.8) shows that the acceleration f is proportional to x, since ω is constant. The negative sign in the right hand side of the equation indicates that the acceleration is directed opposite to the displacement.

Amplitude: The maximum displacement of a particle from its equilibrium position or mean position is its amplitude, and its direction is always away from the mean or equilibrium position. Its S.I. unit is the meter, and the dimensions are $[L^1M^0 T^0]$.

Period: The time taken by a particle to complete one oscillation is its period. Therefore, the period of S.H.M. is the least time after which the motion will repeat itself. Thus, the motion will repeat itself after nT, where, n is an integer.

Frequency: Frequency of S.H.M. is the number of oscillations that a particle performs per unit time. The S.I. unit of frequency is hertz or r.p.s (rotations per second), and its dimensions are $[L^0M^0T^{-1}]$.

Phase: Phase of S.H.M. is its state of oscillation, and the magnitude and direction of displacement of particles represent the phase. Epoch (α) is the phase at the beginning of the motion.

1.6 Total Mechanical Energy of the Particle Executing SHM is Constant:

Total energy E of a particle executing SHM is the sum of kinetic energy (KE) and potential energy (PE).

Using equation 1.7 kinetic energy (KE) can be derived as,

$$KE = \frac{1}{2}mv^2$$

$$KE = \frac{1}{2}ma^2\omega^2 Cos^2\omega t$$

1.9

Using equation 1.6 kinetic energy (KE) can be derived as;

$$PE = \frac{1}{2}kx^2$$

$$PE = \frac{1}{2}ma^2\omega^2 Sin^2\omega t$$

1.10

Hence the total energy E of a particle executing SHM can be written as,

$$E = KE + PE$$

$$E = \frac{1}{2}ma^2\omega^2 Cos^2\omega t + \frac{1}{2}ma^2\omega^2 Sin^2\omega t$$

$$E = \frac{1}{2}ma^2\omega^2$$

1.11

And hence constant.

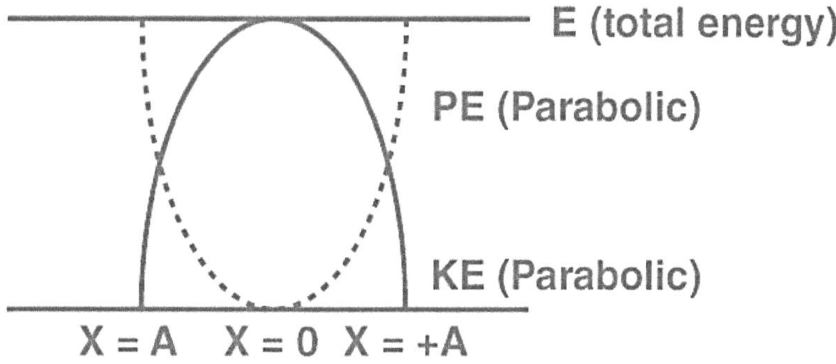

Figure 1.2: Variation of kinetic energy and potential energy with displacement.

1.7 Study of vibrations of cantilever and determination of its time period

Derivation of equation for period of cantilever beam when the distance between the point at which a mass is attached and the pivot changes:

If the mass of the beam is negligible w.r.t. the other mass, it's possible to build a model with only one degree of freedom, resulting in a simple harmonic oscillator. It's possible to split the dynamical system in 2 subsystems: the beam, and the mass; these subsystems are connected by force condition (3rd principle of dynamics) and by the kinematic condition (the displacement of the mass is the same as the displacement of the beam tip).

Beam. If the mass of the beam is negligible, the beam has static response. If it's so, we can build a mathematical model and evaluating the stiffness of the beam using only principles and tools that you could already know at the high school: equilibrium and ordinary derivatives and integrals of powers.

Equilibrium provides the link between the tip force F exchanged with the mass and the internal bending moment in the beam M(x)=−F(ℓ−x). Bernoulli-Euler beam model links the bending moment to the second order derivative of the transverse displacement of the beam w(x),

$$M(x) = EJw''(x)$$

1.12

through the bending stiffness as the combination of the elastic modulus of the material E? and the inertial of the section J. Performing the integration, as shown below, we can link the displacement of the free end of the beam w(ℓ) to the force F,

$$F = \frac{-EJ}{3l^3} w(l)$$

1.13

Mass. The dynamic of the mass is governed by the 2nd principle of Newton's mechanics

$$m\frac{d^2x}{dt^2} = F$$

1.14

and using the expression of F already from the beam, and recalling that w(ℓ)=x , we get the equation of a harmonic oscillator,

$$m\frac{d^2x}{dt^2} + \frac{EJ}{3l^3} w(l) = 0$$

1.15

with pulsation

$$\Omega = \sqrt{\frac{K}{m}} = \sqrt{\frac{3EJ}{ml^3}}$$

1.16

and period

$$T = \frac{2\pi}{\Omega} = 2\pi\sqrt{\frac{ml^3}{3EJ}}$$

1.17

The moment of inertia J of a beam J=1/12 bh³ for a beam with rectangular section, we get the expression for the time period

$$T = \frac{2\pi}{\Omega} = 2\pi\sqrt{\frac{4ml^3}{Ebh^3}}$$

1.18

1.8 Free, Damped and Forced vibrations:

A mechanical system may vibrate in transverse, longitudinal or torsional modes. For example, the motion of a pendulum bob is transverse that of a stretched, spring is longitudinal, while the oscillatory motion of a twisted wire carrying a load at the free end is torsional. Now is all the above three cases, if the systems are displaced from their mean position or state of equilibrium and left to vibrate, then it will keep on oscillating for indefinite time with a constant amplitude and a constant frequency of vibration such a vibration which takes place only under the action of its own elastic force is called natural or free vibration. Such or vibration is an ideal one free from frictional or dissipative force, thus there are no non-conservative forces, and so the total mechanical energy is constant. The frequency of natural vibration depends on the size, mass and elasticity of the body.

Damped Vibration: Damped Vibration refers to the phenomenon where the amplitude of a vibrating system decreases over time due to the presence of a damping force. This force, also known as a damping coefficient, opposes the system's motion and causes the vibration's energy to be dissipated. Damped vibrations are commonly observed in mechanical systems, such as bridges and buildings, and in electrical and electronic systems, such as circuits and filters.

Real vibrating systems are under some dissipative forces. Therefore oscillations die out with time, i.e. amplitude of vibration gradually diminishes with time and ultimately becomes zero. The decrease in amplitude, caused by dissipative forces is called damping, and the corresponding motion is called damped vibration.

The simplest case to analyse damped vibration in detail is a simple harmonic oscillator with a friction or damping force that is directly proportional to the velocity of the oscillating body. The damping force is resent in friction occurring in viscous fluid flow, such as in shock absorbers, similarly resistance in case of an electrical circuit is an example of damping force.

Thus two types of forces act on the vibrating body under damped SHMS:

(a) Restoring force proportioned to displacement and

(b) Damping or retarding force proportional to velocity. The restoring force is therefore equal to - kx where k is the restoring force per unit displacement.

Two simple examples are

(i) The motion of damped harmonic oscillators, i.e. motion of pendulum and

(ii) Moving coil of a galvanometer.

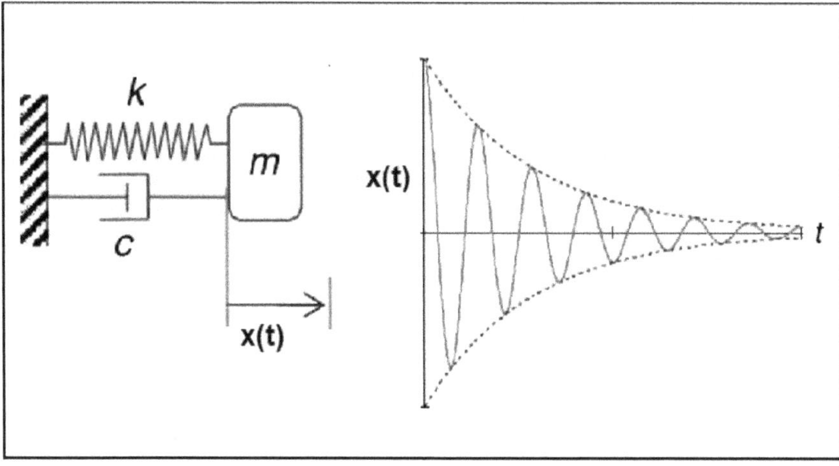

Fig 1.3 shows the examples of damped vibrations.

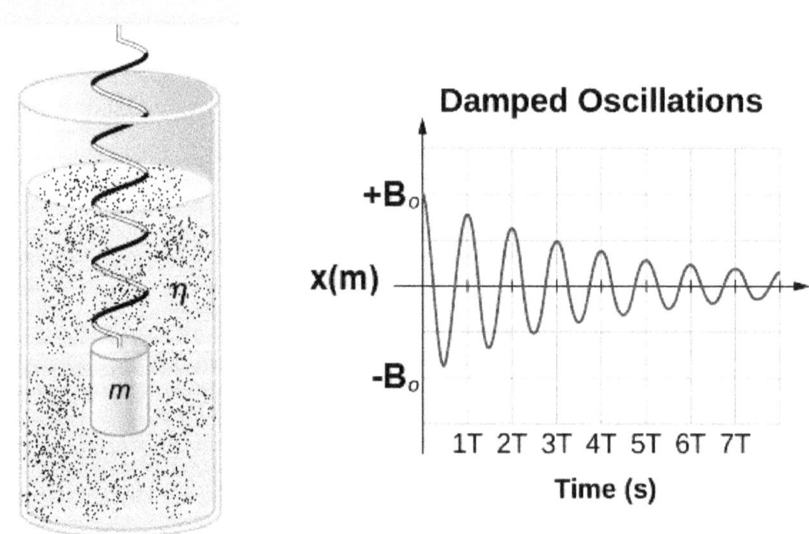

Fig 1.4 shows the examples of damped vibrations.

Forced Vibration: When a vibration takes place under the influence of external periodic force in which the body vibrates with a frequency equal to the frequency of an external periodic force other than its own natural frequency then it is called a forced vibration.

For example: When the wire of a sitar or a guitar is plucked, its board and wind box make forced vibrations. If you were to take a guitar string and stretch it to a given length and a given tightness and have a friend pluck it, you would hear a noise; but the noise would not even be close in comparison to the loudness produced by an acoustic guitar. On the other hand, if the string is attached to the sound box of the guitar, the vibrating string is capable of forcing the sound box into vibrating at that same natural frequency. The sound box in turn forces air particles inside the box into vibrational motion at the same natural frequency as the string. The entire system (string, guitar, and enclosed air) begins vibrating and forces surrounding air particles into vibrational motion. The tendency of one object to force another adjoining or interconnected object into vibrational motion is referred to as a forced vibration. In the case of the guitar string mounted to the sound box, the fact that the surface area of the sound box is greater than the surface area of the string means that more surrounding air particles will be forced into vibration. This causes an increase in the amplitude and thus loudness the sound.

If the tuning fork is held in your hand and hit with a rubber mallet, a sound is produced as the tines of the tuning fork set surrounding air particles into vibrational motion. The sound produced by the tuning fork is barely audible to students in the back rows of the room. However, if the tuning fork is set upon the whiteboard panel or the glass panel of the overhead projector, the panel begins vibrating at the same natural frequency of the tuning fork. The tuning fork forces surrounding glass (or vinyl) particles into vibrational motion. The vibrating whiteboard or overhead projector panel in turn forces surrounding air particles into vibrational motion and the result is an increase in the amplitude and thus loudness of the sound. This principle of forced vibration explains why demonstration tuning forks are mounted on a sound box, why a commercial music box mechanism is mounted on a sounding board, why a guitar utilizes a sound box, and why a piano string is attached to a sounding board. A louder sound is always produced when an accompanying object of greater surface area is forced into vibration at the same natural frequency.

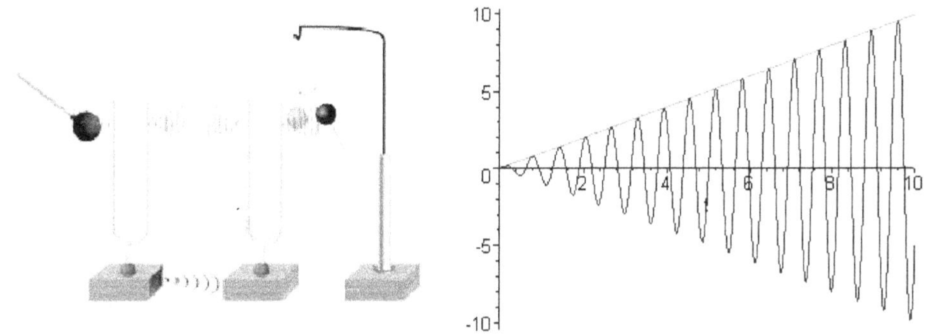

Fig 1.5 Example of Forced vibration.

1.9 Numerical Problem and Solutions

1. Calculate the amplitude, angular frequency, frequency, time period and initial phase for the simple harmonic oscillation given below

a. y = 0.4 sin (40πt + 2.1) b. y = 7 cos (πt) c. y = 3 sin (2πt – 2.5)

Solution-

a. For wave **y = 0.4 sin (40πt + 1.1)**

Amplitude is 0.4 unit.

Angular frequency ω=**40π** rad/s

Frequency f= ω/2π=**40π** /2π=**20** Hz.

Time period T=1/f=1/20=0.05 sec.

Initial phase φ=2.1 rad.

b. For wave **y = 7 cos (πt)**

Amplitude is 7 unit.

Angular frequency ω=π rad/s

Frequency f= ω/2π=π /2π=**0.5** Hz.

Time period T=1/f=1/0.5=2 sec.

Initial phase ϕ=0 rad.

c. For wave **y = 3 sin (2πt – 2.5)**

Amplitude is 3 unit.

Angular frequency ω=2π rad/s

Frequency f= ω/2π= 2π /2π=1 Hz.

Time period T=1/f=1/1=1 sec.

Initial phase ϕ=2.5 rad.

2. A particle of mass 0.5 kg is executing SHM of amplitude 0.03m. When the particle passes through the mean position its kinetic energy is 10 × 10 $^{-3}$J. Obtain the equation of motion of this particle of the initial phase of oscillation in 45°?

Solution-

Equation of motion of a particle in simple harmonic motion is

Given, x=ACos(ωt + Φ)

Amplitude A=0.3 m

Initial phase Φ =45° =π /4 rad

Mass of the particle m =0.5 kg

Kinetic energy at the mean position E_k=10 × 10^{-3}J

$$\frac{1}{2}m\omega^2 A^2 = 10\times10^{-3}$$

$$\omega^2 = \frac{10\times10^{-3}\times2}{0.5\times0.3^2} = 444.4\times10^{-3}$$

$$= 0.67\ s{-}1$$

∴ The equation of motion x = 0.3Cos(0.67t + π /4).

3. An object of mass 3 kg is attached to a spring with spring constant k = 280N/m and is executing simple harmonic motion when the object is 0.02m from its equilibrium position it is moving with a speed of 0.55m/s. Calculate the amplitude of the motion and maximum velocity attained by the object?

Solution-

Mass of the object m= 3 kg

Spring constant k=280 N/m

Displacement x=0.02m

Speed of the object v=0.055m/s

Amplitude of motion A=?

Maximum Velocity Vmax=?

Applying the law of conservation of energy at the point x = 0.02m, we have

$$\frac{1}{2}mv^2 + \frac{1}{2}kx^2 = \frac{1}{2}kA^2$$

$$A^2 = \frac{mv^2 + kx^2}{k}$$

$$A^2 = \frac{3 \times 0.55^2 + 280 \times 0.02^2}{280} = 36.4 \times 10^{-4}$$

$$A = 6 \times 10^{-2}\,m$$

$$v_{max} = A\omega = A\sqrt{\frac{k}{m}} = 6 \times 10^{-2}\sqrt{\frac{280}{3}} = 0.58\,m/s$$

Enter Caption

4. The periodic time of a body executing S.H.M. is 2 s. After how much time interval from t =0 will its displacement be half the amplitude?

Solution-

Given: Time period = T = 2 s, Displacement x = 1/2 a, particle passes through mean position, α = 0.

To Find: Time elapsed = t =?

Angular velocity = ω = 2π/T = 2π/2 = π rad/s

Displacement of a particle performing S.H.M. is given by

x = a sin (ωt + α)

or 1/2 a = a sin (πt + 0)

or 1/2 =sin (πt)

πt = sin^{-1}(1/2) = π/6

Hence t = 1/6 sec.

5. A particle executes S.H.M. of period 12 s and of amplitude 8 cm. What time will it take to travel 4 cm from the extreme position?

Solution-

Given: Period = T = 12 s, amplitude = a = 8cm, distance from extreme position = 4 cm, displacement = x = 8 cm – 4 cm = 4 cm, particle starts from extreme position, α = π/2.

To Find: time taken = t =? Velocity = v = ?

Angular velocity = ω = 2π/T = 2π/12 = π/6 rad/s

Displacement of a particle performing S.H.M. is given by

x = a sin (ωt + α)

4 = 8 sin ((π/6)t + π/2)

1/2 =cos ((π/6)t)

(π/6)t = cos-1(1/2) = π/3

t = 2 sec.

6. The shortest distance travelled by a particle performing S.H.M. from its mean position in 2 seconds is equal to $\sqrt{3}/2$ of its amplitude. Find its period.

Solution-

Given: Time elapsed = t = 2s, displacement = x = a √3/2, particle passes through mean position, α = 0. To Find: Period = T =?

Displacement of a particle performing S.H.M. is given by

x = a sin (ωt + α)

a √3/2 = a sin (ωt + 0)

√3/2 = sin ωt

ωt = sin⁻¹(√3/2) = π/3

(2π/T)t = π/3

(2π/T)x 2 = π/3

T = 2 x 2 x 3 = 12 s

1.10 Objective Type questions with solution

1. Which of the following variables has zero value at the extreme position in SHM?

a) Acceleration b) Speed c) Displacement d) Angular frequency

Answer: b

2. A particle is undergoing SHM with amplitude 10cm. The maximum speed it achieves is 1m/s. Find the time it takes to reach from the mean position to half the amplitude.

a) π/60 s b) π/30 s c) π/15 s d) π/40 s

Answer: a

3. Particles undergoing SHM start from the mean position and go in opposite directions. Particle 1 starts with a speed of 10m/s and particle 2 starts with a speed 0f 5m/s. If the amplitude (=10cm) is the same. At what position will they first meet?

a) 0.0866m b) -0.0633m c) 0 d) 0.0633m

Answer: a

4. A particle has an equation of motion given by: x = cos²wt − sin²wt. Select the correct statement regarding the same.

a) It is not a SHM b) It is a SHM with T = π/w

c) It is an SHM with T = 2π/w d) Amplitude of motion is 1/√2 m

Answer: b

5. A particle starts from the extreme position, at t = 0, in a SHM. If the time period of motion is 2s & maximum speed is 5m/s, find the equation of motion.

a) x = 1.59cos(πt) b) x = 1.59sin(πt) c) x = 2.5sin(2t) d) x = 2.5cos(2t)

Answer: a

6. What is the amplitude of motion for x = 2sin(2t) + 4sin²t ?

a) 2√2 m b) 4 m c) 2 m d) The given equation is not that of an SHM

Answer: a

7. In SHM, what is the phase difference between velocity and acceleration?

a) 0 b) π c) π/2 d) π/3

Answer: c

8. In an SHM the time taken to go from mean position to A/2 is the same as that from A/2 to A. True or False? Here, A is the amplitude of motion.

a) True b) False

Answer: b

9. Every periodic motion is oscillatory, but not vice versa. True or False?

a) True b) False

Answer: b

10. Which of the following describes circular motion?

a) Periodic b) Oscillatory c) Simple Harmonic d) Rectilinear motion

Answer: a

11. In SHM, force at extreme position is zero. True or False?

a) True b) False

Answer: b

12. A ball is thrown up with a velocity of 2.5m/s. It collides elastically with the ground. Find the frequency of this periodic motion.

a) 1Hz b) 2Hz c) 3Hz d) 0.5Hz

Answer: b

13. A function has the equation Acos3t + Bsin3t. Find the value of time period.

a) $\pi/3$ b) $2\pi/3$ c) $A\pi/3 + B\pi/3$ d) $\pi/3A + \pi/3B$

Answer: b

14. What is the frequency of SHM?

a) Number of oscillations per unit time b) Time for one oscillation

c) Time taken for motion to reverse direction d) Same as angular frequency

Answer: a

15. Force on a particle is given by: $F = -kx^n$. For what values of n will the motion be oscillatory?

a) 3 b) 4 c) Any integer d) It cannot be oscillatory for any value of n

Answer: a

16. In SHM, force at extreme position is zero. True or False?

a) True b) False

Answer: b

17. In damped vibrations, the amplitude of the resulting vibration gradually reduces. This is due to the reason that an amount of energy is always dissipated to overcome the _________

a) Frictional resistance b) Work done c) Fluid pressure d) Air pressure

Answer: a

18. The resistance to the motion of the body is provided by _______

a) Medium of vibration b) Speed of vibration c) Length of the material d) External friction

Answer: a

19. In which direction does the damping force acts?

a) Opposite to the motion b) Along the motion c) Perpendicular to motion d) Variable

Answer: a

20. In which direction does the accelerating force acts?

a) Opposite to the motion b) Along the motion c) Perpendicular to motion d) Variable

Answer: b

21. In forced vibrations, the magnitude of damping force at resonance is equal to the impressed force.

a) Correct b) Incorrect c) Can't say d) Not always

Answer: a

1.11 Important Questions:

1. Define Simple Harmonic Motion. Explain that all periodic motion is not a simple harmonic motion.
2. Derive the differential equation of Simple Harmonic Motion and hence solve it.
3. Show that the total energy is conserved for a particle executing Simple Harmonic Motion.
4. At what displacement from equilibrium is the energy of a simple harmonic oscillator half P.E and half K.E?
5. Derive the expression of time period of vibrations of cantilever.

6. If a mass of 10 g is hung from a suspended spring, it elongates by 2mm. If the spring is pulled a little downwards and then released, what will be the frequency of vibration of the spring?

7. A particle of mass 10 g is placed in a potential field given by $v=(50x^2+100)$ erg/g. Calculate the frequency of oscillation.

8. Two particles are executing simple harmonic motions with equal frequency and amplitude. When the displacements of the two particles are half of their amplitudes, they cross each other in mutually opposite directions. What is the phase difference of their vibrations?

9. A simple pendulum is formed by hanging a sphere of mass of 1 kg from a copper wire of length 5 m and of diameter, 0.08 cm and then the time period of this pendulum is measured. Now the sphere of mass 1 kg is replaced by another sphere of mass 10 kg. Determine the change in time period of the pendulum. [Y for copper = 12.4×10^{10} N/m^2]

10. A solid sphere of radius R is floating in a liquid of density ρ with half of its volume submerged. If the sphere is slightly pushed and released, it starts performing simple harmonic motion. Find the frequency of these oscillations.

Chapter -2: Wave motion and its applications

Chapter -2: Wave motion and its applications

2.1 Introduction:

Wave Motion is the motion of the waves. A wave is defined as a disturbance caused by the propagation of energy in space or a medium. The ripples in water, the propagation of sound, the rays of light, are all examples of wave motion. In this article, we will study the different types of waves in nature and their wave motion.

2.2 Functions of Waves

Wave Motion can perform the following functions.

1. Transfer Energy
2. Transfer Information
3. Cause disturbance in the media

All waves have characteristic features which are called properties of waves. These properties of the waves define wave motion. Wave Motion can be defined by Amplitude, Frequency, Wavelength, Time Period, Phase and Phase Difference.

Speed of a Travelling Wave Motion
Wave Speed is given by
Wave Speed=distance covered / time taken
In order to describe the phase at a place, we need to know

1. displacement
2. the direction of velocity and
3. the oscillation number (during which oscillation) of the particle there

Number of Dimensions a Wave Propagates Energy
Waves can exist in two or three dimensions. For example, a plane wave is where the wavefront or crest of the wave makes a line (in two dimensions) or a plane (in three dimensions). Circular waves (in two dimensions) and spherical waves (in three dimensions) also exist.

2.3 Periodic Wave Motion

When a motion is repeated in equal intervals of time. Waves that can be represented by sine curves are periodic. A periodic wave is one that repeats as a function of both time and position and can be described by its amplitude, frequency, wavelength, speed, and energy. A periodic wave repeats the same oscillation for several cycles, such as in the case of the wave pool, and is associated with simple harmonic motion.

The Relationship between Path Difference and Phase Difference

Path difference is the difference in the path traversed by the two waves, measured in terms of its wavelength. Path difference has a direct relation with the phase difference of the wave. Phase difference decides the nature of the interference pattern but phase difference is found out by path difference. The phase difference is related to quantum mechanics. If path difference b/w two waves are even multiple of the half-wavelength, which satisfies the condition for constructive interference. Whereas, if path difference b/w two waves are an odd multiple of half-wavelength, it satisfies the condition for destructive interference.

The Terminologies mentioned below are applicable for all types of waves:

1. Amplitude (A): The maximum displacement of a particle of the medium from its mean position is called Amplitude. Its S.I unit is a meter.
2. Time period (T): The time required to complete one complete oscillation to and fro about its mean position by a particle of the medium is the time period T of the wave. It is measured in seconds.
3. Wavelength (λ): The distance between two successive crests or troughs for a wave is termed wavelength. Its S.I unit is a meter.
4. Frequency (n): The number of oscillations performed by a particle in one sec is termed the frequency of waves. Its S.I unit is Hertz (Hz). Frequency is the reciprocal of the time period i.e., F=1/T
5. Velocity (v): The distance covered by a wave per unit of time is called the velocity of the wave. During the period (T), the wave covers a distance equal to the wavelength (λ) Thus, the magnitude of the velocity of the wave is given as, i.e., velocity of wave (v)= Frequency (n)× Wavelength (λ)
6. Phase: The state of oscillation of a particle is called its phase.

2.4 Classification of Wave Motion

Depending upon the wave motion, these waves can be classified into three types.

Mechanical Waves

The wave which can only be propagated in a material medium is termed as mechanical waves (need some medium for the propagation of wave motion).

Examples: water waves, waves along a stretched string, seismic waves (earthquake), sound waves.

Electromagnetic Waves

The waves which are caused because of the oscillating electric and magnetic field are termed electromagnetic waves. These waves don't require any medium for the propagation of wave motion.

Examples: Light waves (Photon)

Matter Waves

The wave motion that is associated with the motion of particles like electrons, protons, etc. are termed matter waves.

Standing Wave Motion

A standing wave or stationary wave is a special type of wave which oscillates within a confined space. The crest and trough of a standing wave do not move in space. The oscillations at different points in a standing wave are in phase with each other. In short, this sort of wave motion does not propagate in space

Examples: Motion of Strings of a Sitar

Wave Speed of a Wave Motion on a Stretched String

The velocity of a standing wave in a stretched string is determined by the tension and the mass per unit length of the string.

$$v = \sqrt{\frac{T}{mL}}$$

2.1

Progressive Wave Motion

The waves which propagate in a media are called Progressive waves. The crest and trough of a progressive wave do move in space.

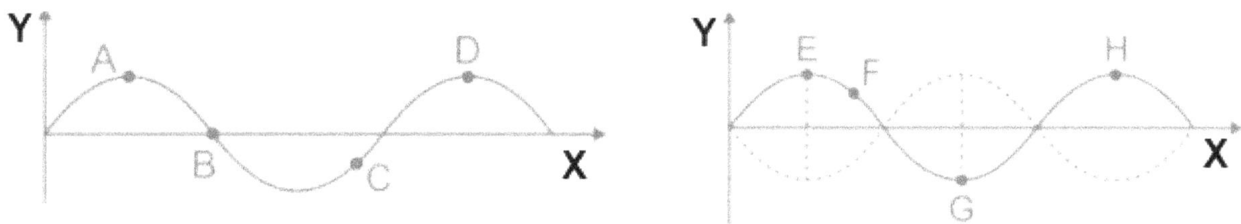

Figure 2.1 shows, progressive and standing waves as a displacement along x and y-axis and the different points on the graph show the phase change of the particle.

Types of Progressive Waves

The progressive waves can be classified into two types:

1. Longitudinal Wave Motion
2. Transverse Wave Motion

Longitudinal Wave Motion

Longitudinal waves are the waves in which the particle of the medium vibrates parallel to the direction of its propagation of wave motion.

Sound waves are the best example of longitudinal waves.

Transverse Wave Motion

Transverse waves are the waves in which the particle of the medium vibrates perpendicular to the direction of its propagation of wave motion.

Water ripple is an example of a transverse wave in which water molecules vibrate perpendicular to the surface of the water while the wave propagates along the surface.

In transverse waves, particles of the medium vibrate up and down in the vertical direction whereas it is propagating along the horizontal direction. Hence in a transverse wave motion, a crest is a part where a particle rises from its mean position whereas a trough is a part where a particle dips below the mean position.

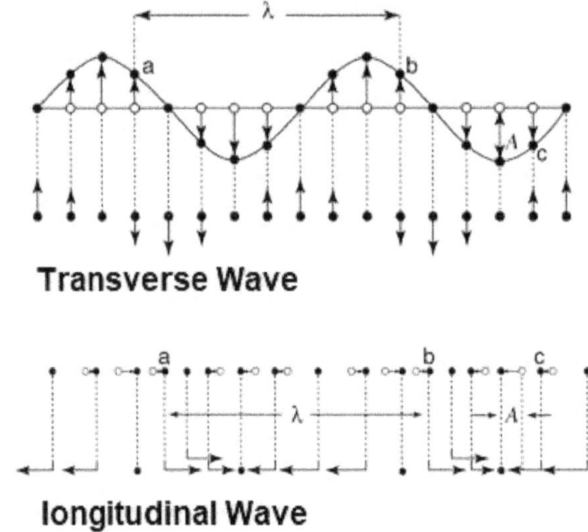

Figure 2.2 illustrates the wavelength (λ) and the amplitude for both transverse and longitudinal waves.

2.5 Wave Equation

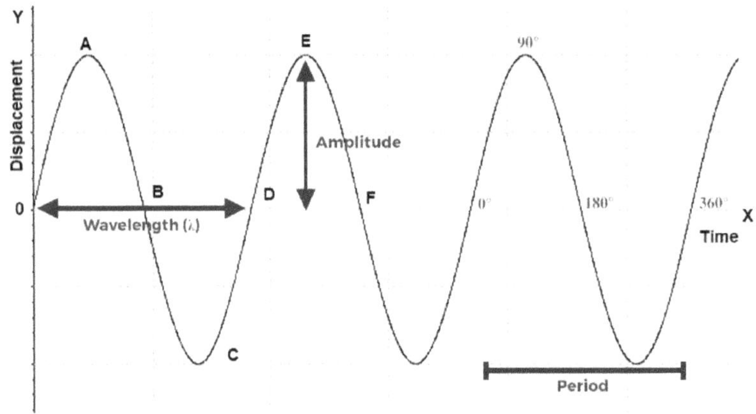

Fig 2.3 Displacement of wave as a function of time

A wave starting from origin O. At any instant of time t the displacement of the wave motion is

y=aSinwt 2.2

Where 'a' is the amplitude. A second wave starts behind the first wave. It lags by a difference of Θ. The displacement of this wave at time t is given by,

y=aSin(wt-Θ) 2.3

We know that path difference corresponds to a phase difference of 2π. Therefore, a path difference of 'x' will correspond to a phase difference of $2\pi x/\lambda$.

$$y = a\,Sin\left(\omega t - \frac{2\pi x}{\lambda}\right)$$

2.4

This is called the Wave Equation. It gives the position of any particle at any instant of time for a particular wave motion.

Energy and Power of a Wave Motion Traveling Along a String

Potential Energy and Kinetic Energy can be given by

$$PE = \frac{1}{4}m\omega^2 a^2 \lambda$$

2.5

$$KE = \frac{1}{4}m\omega^2 a^2 \lambda$$

2.6

Hence the Total energy will be

$$E = KE + PE = \frac{1}{4}m\omega^2 a^2 \lambda + \frac{1}{4}m\omega^2 a^2 \lambda$$

$$E = \frac{1}{2}m\omega^2 a^2 \lambda$$

2.7

Speed of Longitudinal Waves According to Newton's Formula

Now according to Newton's formula, the velocity of a longitudinal wave motion or a pulse depends upon the properties of the medium like its density and elasticity.

If the medium is uniform or unchanging, then the velocity of sound remains constant and it can be expressed as:

$$\upsilon = \sqrt{\frac{Elastic\ Property}{Internal\ Property}} = \sqrt{\frac{B}{\rho}}$$

2.8

Here, B is the bulk modulus of medium and ρ is the density of the medium.

Bulk modulus: The bulk modulus is a constant that describes how resistant a substance is to compression. It is defined as the proportion of volumetric stress related to the volumetric strain of any specified material.

For example: Speed of sound depends upon bulk modulus of material and density of the material, as we know that Saltwater is about 2-4% denser than freshwater. But it also has a bulk modulus that's about 9% greater than that of freshwater. So overall the speed of sound in seawater is faster than tap water/freshwater.

Speed of Longitudinal Waves (Sound) According to Laplace's Correction

Using Newton's assumption Laplace pointed out that it will not give correct results as it is considered for an ideal condition. According to Laplace, the pressure-volume changes that occur when a sound wave travels through the gas are not isothermal but they must be adiabatic in nature. He assumed that there is no heat exchange taking place as the sound propagates through air.

Hence according to Laplace's correction formula for the speed of sound in a gas is

$$\upsilon = \sqrt{\frac{\gamma P}{\rho}}$$

2.9

Factors Affecting the Speed of Wave Motion:

1. Elasticity: Elastic properties relate to the tendency of a material to maintain its shape and not deform when a force is applied to it. Elastic materials have closely bonded atoms and hence the speed of the wave motion is more in an elastic material.
2. Density: Density describes the mass of the substance per unit volume. If the material is denser because its molecules are larger, it will transmit waves slower.
3. Temperature: The wave motion travels faster in a warm environment than in a cold environment. Elasticity and Density are the properties of the medium
4. Humidity: In a humid environment, the wave motion travels faster as compared to the dry environment.
5. The direction of wind: The direction of wind greatly affects the speed of the wave motion, for example, if the wave is propagating in the direction of wind flow its speed will increase whereas if the wave is propagating in the opposite direction of wind flow its speed will decrease greatly.

2.6 Superposition principle

If two waves pass through the same region of space, they combine by a process called superposition. The superposition principle is that the resultant wave formed by the simultaneous influence of two or more waves is the vector sum of the displacements due to each wave acting independently. If two pulses of the same size and shape on the same side of the rope arrive at a given point at the same time, they will—for an instant—combine to form a pulse that is twice the size of each of the individual pulses. This is called constructive interference. If the same two pulses are on opposite sides of the string. In this case, the two pulses will momentarily cancel each other out. This is called destructive interference.

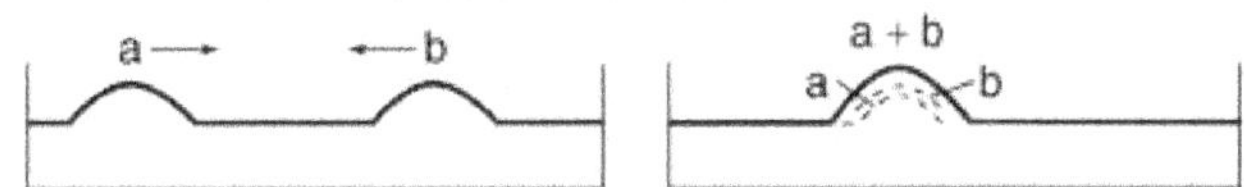

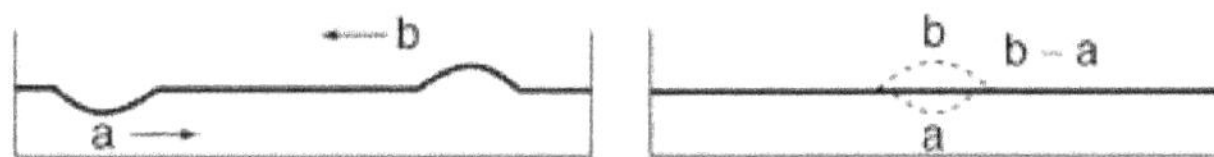

Fig 2.4 Constructive interference and destructive interference

Interference and Beats

When two or more waves travelling in a medium meet, the resulting phenomenon is called interference and beats are an excellent example of the phenomenon of interference. The superimposed waves (having slight variation in their frequencies) have an alternating loudness and softness; this fluctuation is a beat.

The Application of Beats

There are various applications of beats, though the three are discussed in detail below.

1. Beats are used in determining the unknown frequency
2. Beats are used in determining the existence of poisonous gases in mines.
3. To identify the presence of poisonous gases in the mine, the following experiment is carried out. Two pipes equal in size are taken, and one is filled with the pure ai. The other pipe is filled with the air in the mine. The pipes are blown together. The pipe that consists of pure air does not produce any sound whereas if some amount of sound is produced by the pipe that consists of mine air, then it indicates the presence of poisonous gases. If the beats are produced, then the mine air is not pure.
4. Beats are used in determining the tone of musical instruments.
5. Two musical instruments are sounded together to notice if two instruments vibrate in a similar tone. If the tones of both the instruments are similar, then no beats will be heard. In such a way, the tones of various musical instruments can be adjusted according to the beats.
6. Beats are used to adjust the vibrating length between two bridges in the sonometer experiment.
7. Based on the phenomenon of the beats, the doppler ultrasonography and echocardiography works.
8. The aeroplane speed can be determined by the Doppler RADAR. This is based on the phenomenon of beats.

Beat Frequency

If the frequency of a wave is f_1, and that of another wave is f_2. So, the frequency of the beat is the difference between these two, which is:

$$f_{BEATS} = |f_1 - f_2| \quad 2.10$$

2.7 Acoustics of buildings- Reverberation

In any architectural environment, as sound is emitted in any form it takes time to dissipate. However long it takes for that single sound to become inaudible is what the reverberation time is.

Now, onto the science bit. There are many elements to a space that can increase or decrease the reverberation time. What prolongs the sound is how many times the sound wave can reflect off surfaces in the room. More hard, shiny, flat surfaces in a space the more likely a longer reverberation time than a room that's fluffy floor to ceiling.

As sound continues to reflect and reverberate, noise builds up. This is why reverberation in a room impacts speech intelligibility (understanding) and the quality of sound, due to the muffled and repeatedly bounced-around sound waves.

Sound is caused by vibrations which transmit through a medium such as air and reach the ear or some other form of detecting device. Sound intensity is measured in Decibels (dB). This is a logarithmic scale in which an increase of 10 dB gives an apparent doubling of loudness.

Resistance to the passage of sound defines 'Reverberation' as the persistence of sound in a space after a sound source has been stopped. Reverberation time is the time, in seconds, taken for the sound to decay by 60dB after a sound source has been stopped.

The reverberation time of a room is linked to the surfaces that enclose it and the volume of the room by the Sabine equation:

RT = Volume x 0.161 / Total Acoustic Absorption 2.11

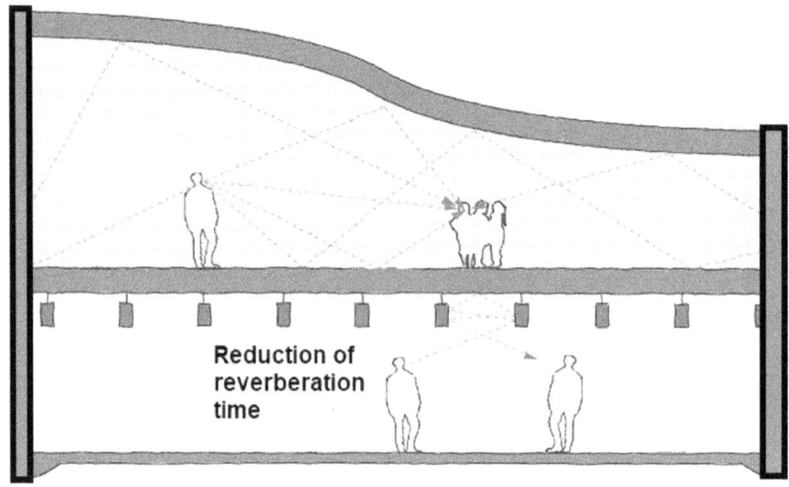

Fig 2.5 Reduction of reverberation

Factors affecting acoustics of buildings and their remedies

The factors affecting acoustics of buildings and their remedies are as follows:

1. Reverberation time:

If the reverberation time is very small, the sound intensity decreases very fast and makes the sound appear dead. On the other hand, a large reverberation time causes mixing of different syllables and hence causes confusion. For good quality sound, optimum reverberation time is required.

Remedies:

i) Heavy curtains with folds are used to reduce reverberation time by increasing absorption of sound

ii) Floor is covered with carpets to absorb sound.

iii) Windows and openings are provided in the hall which can be opened or closed to control the reverberation time.

iv) Walls and ceilings are covered with sound absorbing materials.

v) If the hall is filled to its maximum capacity of audience, reverberation time is less.

2. Loudness:

There should be adequate loudness in all parts of the hall.

Remedies:

i) Large sounding boards are used behind the speaker facing the audience.

ii) Loudspeakers are used to increase the loudness.

iii) Low ceilings help to reflect the sound towards the audience.

iv) Sound absorbing materials are used in those parts of the hall where sound intensity is large.

(3) Echo:

The reflection of sound from a distant reflecting surface is known as echo. If the echo reaches the listener about 1/15 th of a second after the direct sound, the listener hears two sounds instead of one which causes confusion. Such echoes mush be eliminated in halls.

Remedy:

High ceilings and distant walls are covered with second absorbing materials.

(4) Echelon effect:

Succession of echoes produced by a set of regularly spaced reflecting surfaces like staircase causes confusion in original sound. This effect is known as echelon effect.

Remedy:

The regularly spaced reflecting surfaces like stairs are covered with sound absorbing materials like carpets.

(5) Focusing:

Concave and parabolic surfaces in the hall focus sound. This causes concentration of sound in certain regions of the hall which is not desirable.

Remedies:

Curved surfaces are avoided, If there are curved surfaces, they are covered with sound absorbing materials.

(6) Resonance:

Loose fitting window panels and some other objects resonate at some audible frequencies creating more sound of these frequencies. This distorts the original sound.

Remedies:

Window panels are fixed properly, Vibrating objects are placed on sound absorbing materials.

(7) Noise:

Noise from different sources adversely affects the quality of sound in a hall. The noise can be air borne, structure borne or inside noise.

a) Air borne noise:

The external noise, for example of traffic, which enters the halls through doors, windows and ventilators is known as external noise.

Remedies:

i) Openings for ventilators inside the hall are avoided.

ii) Doors and windows are provided with rubber covering on frames so that they shut without any gaps.

iii) Double doors and windows having separate frames enclosing sound absorbing materials are used.

b) Structure borne noise:

Noise produced by activities like drilling and hammering or the vibrations of heavy machinery is transmitted through the structure of the building. This is known as structure borne noise.

Remedies:

i) Heavy machinery is mounted on sound absorbing materials like wood or rubber.

ii) Double walls are used with space between them.

c) Inside noise:

It is the noise produced inside the hall by machinery, fans, air conditioners etc.

Remedies:

i) Sound absorbing materials and curtains are provided near the sources of noise.

ii) The sources of noise are mounted on sound absorbing materials.

2.8 Ultrasonic waves

Sound wave is a vibration that is transmitted through a medium, such as air, water, and metals. Ultrasonic wave is defined as "inaudible sound with high frequency for human" the frequency of which generally exceeds 20 kHz. These days, sound wave which is not intended to be heard is also called ultrasonic wave. Sound waves with a frequency of more than 20,000 Hz or 20 kHz are called ultrasound waves.

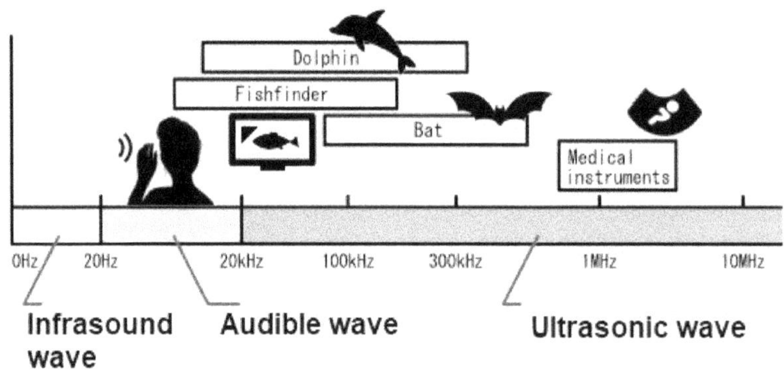

2.6 Ultrasonic waves

Properties of Ultrasound Waves:

1. Ultrasound waves cannot travel through a vacuum.
2. These waves are high-frequency sound waves that have a smaller wavelength.
3. These waves travel with a speed that is equal to that of sound in the given medium.
4. The velocity of ultrasound waves remains constant in homogenous media.

Applications of Ultrasound

Ultrasound is used for various applications. It is useful in various fields of science, medicines, and even in daily practical activities because of its precision in results. Scientists are still discovering even newer applications of ultrasound in the field of medical sciences for conducting minor surgeries and treating patients. Given below are some applications of ultrasound:

Ultrasonography: Ultrasound waves are used to project diagnostic imaging techniques to detect internal problems in the body. In this technique, internal body structures like muscles, bones, internal organs are imaged by passing pulses of ultrasound through the body. The sound hit the tissues issuing probe and echo off. Different issues reflect varying degrees of sound and form the final image. The images produced by ultrasound are called sonograms. Ultrasonography is used the most by doctors to check on a developing baby.

Crack Detection: Ultrasound is used for crack detection in metallic components used in the construction of buildings and high-rise structures. The waves generate and display a type of ultrasonic waveform that is studied by a trained operator to locate and categorize cracks or flaws, often through the medium of analysis software. Since these waves have a very high frequency. they reflect from cracks and fissures in predictable ways, thus forming distinct echo patterns. These patterns are easily displayed and recorded on portable instruments. Trained operators identify specific patterns corresponding to the echoes produced from the good parts and the flawed parts.

Echocardiography: Another application of ultrasound in the medical field is Echocardiography or ECG. This is also an imagining technique used to detect a patient's heart condition. Ultrasonic waves are used in this technique to produce reflections from various parts of the heart and detect diseases

Lithotripsy: Ultrasonic waves are also used to break kidney stones. High energy sound waves are passed directly through the body that breaks the stones into small pieces without causing any injury. These fragmented stones move through the urinary tracts and are eliminated from the body easily.

Cleaning and Clearing: Ultrasound is very helpful in cleaning objects like spiral tubes or electronic components, that have parts difficult to reach normally. In this process, the desired objects are put in a cleaning solution and ultrasonic waves are passed through it. The high frequency of these waves causes the grease and dirt to detach from the surface, thus cleaning them easily.

Echolocation: One of the most important usages of ultrasound is in the process of echolocation, where sound waves are used to determine the movement of objects in the space. Echolocation is also the technique used by bats to navigate smoothly through the dark. Bats send out high-frequency sound waves from their mouths and nose that hit close objects like trees or buildings in the dark. These waves then reflect off from the surface. The nature of the echoes produced from these surfaces helps the bats determine the shape and distance of the objects and accordingly navigate through them.

SONAR: Another major application of ultrasound is in the technique of SONAR- Sound Navigation and Ranging. In this process, high-frequency ultrasonic sound waves are passed through water bodies for navigational purposes. The sound waves easily travel underwater and are used for communication and detection. The SONAR is the process of how submarines are detected as well.

2.9 Numerical Problem and Solutions

1. A wave has frequency of 50 Hz and a wavelength of 10 m. What is the speed of the wave?
Solution-
$f=50$ Hz, $\lambda=10$m , $v=?$
$v= \lambda x f=10x50=500$ m/s
2. A wave has frequency of 5 Hz and a speed of 25 m/s. What is the wavelength of the wave?
Solution-
$f=5$ Hz, $v=25$ m/s, $\lambda=?$
$v= \lambda x f$
$\lambda=v/f=25/5=5$ m
3. A wave has wavelength of 10 m and a speed of 340 m/s. What is the frequency of the wave?
Solution-
$\lambda=10$m, $v=340$ m/s, $f=?$
$v= \lambda x f$
$f=v/\lambda=340/10=34$ Hz

2.10 Objective Type questions with solution

1. All waves require material for propagation. True or False?
a) True b) False
Answer: b
2. Transverse waves involve energy transfer by movement of medium particles, while longitudinal waves don't. True or False?
a) True b) False
Answer: b
3. Electromagnetic waves are considered to be which of the following types?
a) Transverse b) Longitudinal c) Both Transverse & Longitudinal
d) neither longitudinal nor transverse
Answer: a
4. What does the given equation: x = Asin(ky+wt+a) represent?
a) Wave travelling along positive x direction b) Wave travelling along negative x direction
c) Wave travelling along positive y direction d) Wave travelling along negative y direction

Answer: d

5. An equation of a wave is given by: y = 2sin(3x-2t+π/2). What is the minimum distance between two points having the same phase?

a) 3 b) π/2 c) 2π/3 d) π

Answer: c

6. A sinusoidal wave has an amplitude of 2cm. It is travelling in the negative x-direction. The distance between two crests is 2cm. The angular frequency is πs-1. What is the displacement of the particle at x = 20.5cm, at t = 10s? Assume that at t=0 & x=0 the particle was at the mean position and going downwards. 'x' &'y' are in cm.

a) 0cm b) 1cm c) -1cm d) -2cm

Answer: d

7. The equation of a wave is given by y = 3sin(4x-2t). What is the time period and wavelength of the wave?

a) T = 2π, λ = 2π b) T = π, λ = 2π c) T = π, λ = π/2 d) T = π/2, λ = π

Answer: c

8. What is the expression for wave speed in the given equation: y = Asin(kx-wt + π)?

a) dy/dt b) w/k c) 2πw/k d) 2πk/w

Answer: b

9. A string has a mass of 100gm & is under a tension of 10N. What should be its length if the speed of transverse waves is to be 10m/s on the string?

a) 1.8m b) 10m c) 1m d) 2m

Answer: c

10. The formula v = √(P/ρ) can be used for any gas considering isothermal process. True or False?

a) True b) False

Answer: b

11. The speed of sound in air is 330m/s. What is the mass of 1 mole of air? Assume it is an ideal gas.

a) 28gm b) 38gm c) 20.56gm d) 29gm

Answer: c

12. What is the ratio of speed of sound in air when measured after laplace correction to that measured by Newton's formula?

a) 1.18 b) 0.84 c) 1.4 d) 0.71

Answer: a

13. Laplace correction makes use of which of the following processes?

a) Isothermal b) Adiabatic c) Isochoric d) Isobaric

Answer: b

14. Two interfering waves have a frequency of 2Hz & 6Hz. What is the beat frequency?

a) 8Hz b) 4Hz c) 2Hz d) 0

Answer: b

15. In a standing wave the amplitude of a particle is fixed, but varies from particle to particle. True or False?

a) True b) False

Answer: a

16. What is the minimum distance between a node & an antinode in a standing wave?

a) λ b) λ/2 c) 2λ d) λ/4

Answer: d

17. If a standing wave is vibrating in the fourth harmonic and the wavelength is λ, what is the length of the string?

a) 2λ b) λ c) 4λ d) λ/4

Answer: a

18. A pipe is open at both ends. What should be its length such that it resonates a 10Hz source in the 2nd harmonic? Speed of sound in air = 340m/s.

a) 34m b) 68m c) 17m d) 51m

Answer: a

19. Consider standing waves in an air column with one end closed. What is a pressure node?

a) Pressure variation is maximum b) Displacement variation is minimum

c) Same as displacement node d) Least pressure change

Answer: d

20. Standing waves can be produced when two identical waves, having a phase difference of π, are travelling in the same direction. True or False?

a) True b) False

Answer: b

21. If a string wave encounters a completely fixed end, what happens to its phase?

a) Stays the same b) Changes by π c) Changes by $\pi/2$ d) Waves gets destroyed

Answer: b

22. In a standing wave the amplitude of a particle is fixed, but varies from particle to particle. True or False?

a) True b) False

Answer: a

23. The velocity of a particle moving with simple harmonic motion is . . . . at the mean position.

a) zero b) minimum c) maximum d) none of the mentioned

Answer: c

2.11 Important Questions:

1. Derive the expression of Energy and Power of a Wave Motion Traveling Along a String.
2. Define Ultrasonic wave. What are the properties of Ultrasonic wave?
3. State the applications of Ultrasonic wave.
4. What are the factors affecting the Speed of Wave Motion?
5. What are the applications of beats?
6. A wave with a frequency of 14 Hz has a wavelength of 3 meters. At what speed will this wave travel?
7. The speed of a wave is 65 m/sec. If the wavelength of the wave is 0.8 meters, what is the frequency of the wave?
8. A wave has a frequency of 46 Hz and a wavelength of 1.7 meters. What is the speed of this wave?
9. A wave traveling at 230 m/sec has a wavelength of 2.1 meters. What is the frequency of this wave?
10. 5. A wave with a frequency of 500 Hz is traveling at a speed of 200 m/s. What is the wavelength?
11. A wave has a frequency of 540 Hz and is traveling at 340 m/s. What is its wavelength?
12. A wave has a wavelength of 125 meters is moving at a speed of 20 m/s. What is it's frequency?
13. A wave has a frequency of 900 Hz and a wavelength of 200 m. At what speed is this wave traveling?
14. A wave has a wavelength of 0.5 meters and a frequency of 120 Hz. What is the wave's speed?

Chapter -3: Ray Optics and its applications

Chapter -3: Ray Optics and its applications

3.1 Introduction:

Optics. It is the branch of physics which deals with the study of nature, production and propagation of light. The subject of optics can be divided into two main branches: rays optics and wave optics.

1. Ray or geometrical optics. It concerns itself with the particle nature of light and is based on (i) the rectilinear propagation of light and (ii) the laws of reflection and refraction of light. It explains the formation of images in mirrors and lenses, the aberrations of optical images and the working and designing of optical instruments.

2. Wave or physical optics. It concerns itself with the wave nature of light and is based on the phenomena like (i) interference, (ii) diffraction and (iii) polarisation of light.

3.2 Behaviour of light at the interface of two media

2. Name the different effects that may occur as light travels from one optical medium to another. State the laws of reflection of light. Behaviour of light at the interface of two media. When light travelling in one medium falls on the surface of a second medium, the following three effects may occur:

(i) A part of the incident light is turned back into the first medium. This is called reflection of light.

(ii) A part of the incident light is transmitted into the second medium along a changed direction. This is called refraction of light.

(iii) The remaining third part of light energy is absorbed by the second medium. This is called absorption of light.

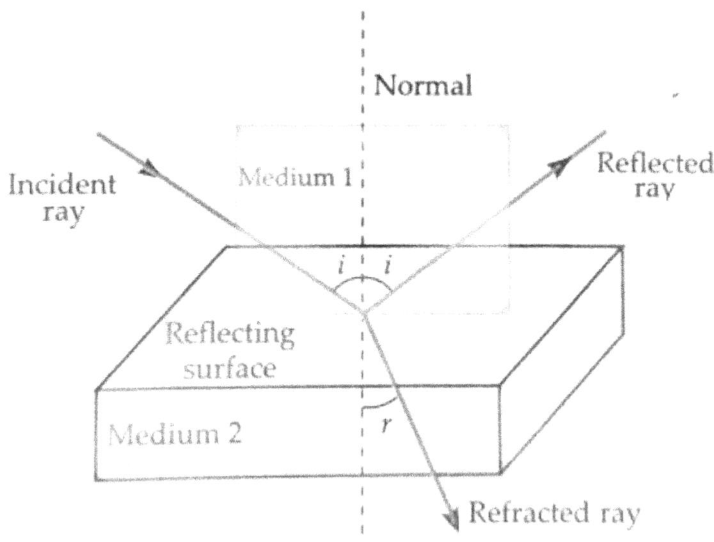

Fig 3.1 reflection & Refraction of light.

3.3 Reflection of light:

Definition: Reflection or Reflection of light is the process of bouncing back light rays when it strikes the smooth and shiny reflecting surface.

Reflection of light takes place according to the following two laws:

(i) The angle of incidence is equal to the angle of reflection, i.e. <i=<r

(ii) The incident ray, the reflected ray and the normal at the point of incidence all lie in the same plane.

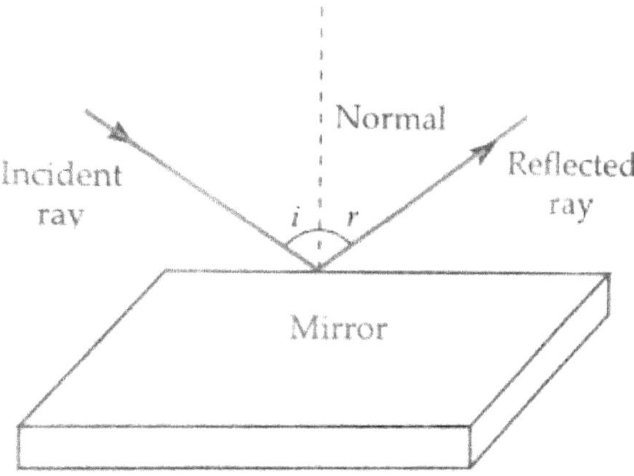

Fig 3.2 Reflection of light

The above laws of reflection are valid both in case of plane and curved reflecting surfaces.

Refraction of light

Definition: When light travels in the same homogeneous medium, it travels along a straight path. However, when it passes obliquely from one transparent medium to another, the direction of its path changes at the interface of the two media. The phenomenon of the change in the path of light as it passes obliquely from one transparent medium to another is called refraction of light.

The path along which the light travels in the first medium is called incident ray and that in the second medium is called refracted ray. The angles which the incident ray and the refracted ray make with the normal at the surface of separation are called angle of incidence (i) and angle of refraction (r) respectively.

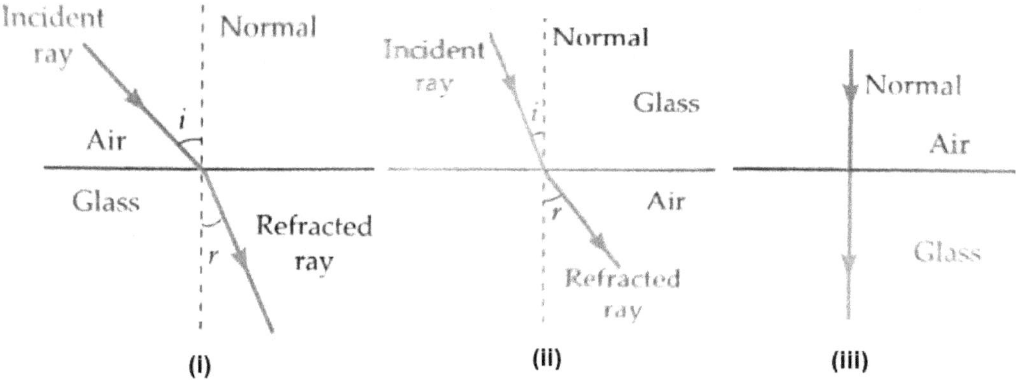

Fig 3.3 Refraction of light

It is observed that

1. When a ray of light passes from an optically rarer medium to a denser medium, it bends towards the normal **r<i** as shown in Fig. 3.3(i)

2. When a ray of light passes from an optically denser to a rarer medium, it bends away from the normal **r>i** as shown in Fig. 3.3(ii)

3. A ray of light travelling along the normal passes un-deflected, as shown in Fig. 3.3(iii) Here $r=i=0^0$

Laws of refraction of light

The phenomenon of refraction of light obeys the following two laws:

First law: The incident ray, the refracted ray and the normal to the interface at the point of incidence all lie in the same plane,

Second law: The ratio of the sine of the angle of incidence and the sine of the angle of refraction is constant for a given pair of media.

Mathematically

3.1

This ratio is called refractive index of second medium with respect to first medium. The second law was first deduced by a Dutch scientist Willibord Snell 1621, so it is also known as Snell's law of refraction.

3.4 Refractive Index

In terms of speed of light the refractive index of a medium may be defined in terms of the speed of light as follows:

The refractive index of a medium for a light of given wavelength may be defined as the ratio of the speed of light in vacuum to its speed in that medium.

$$\text{Refractive index}(\mu) = \frac{\text{Speed of light in vacuum}}{\text{Speed of light in medium}}$$

$$\mu = \frac{c}{v}$$

3.2

Refractive index of a medium with respect to vacuum is also called absolute refractive index. Refractive index in terms of wavelength. Since the frequency (v) remains unchanged when light passes from one medium to another, therefore,

$$\mu = \frac{c}{v} = \frac{\lambda_{vacuum} \times v}{\lambda_{medium} \times v} = \frac{\lambda_{vacuum}}{\lambda_{medium}}$$

3.3

The refractive index of a medium may be defined as the ratio of wavelength of light in vacuum to its wavelength in that medium.

Relative refractive index. The relative refractive index of medium 2 with respect to medium 1 is defined as the ratio of speed of light (v_1) in medium 1 to the speed of light (v_2) in medium 2 and is denoted by:

$$^1\mu_2 = \frac{v_2}{v_2}$$

3.4

As refractive index is the ratio of two similar physical quantities, so it has no units and dimensions.

Factors on which the refractive index of a medium depends.

These are as follows:

1. Nature of the medium,
2. Wavelength of the light used.
3. Temperature.
4. Nature of the surrounding medium.

It may be noted that refractive index is a characteristic of the pair of the media and also depends on the wavelength of light, but is independent of the angle of incidence.

Cause of refraction of light

Light travels with different speeds in different media. The bending of light or refraction occurs due to the change in the speed of light as it passes from one medium to another. Larger the change in the speed of light as it passes from one medium to another, the more is the bending due to refraction. The

Snell's law of refraction may be written as sin

$$^1\mu_2 = \frac{Sin\,i}{Sin\,r} = \frac{v_2}{v_2}$$

3.5

From the above equation, we can note the following results:

(i) If $v_1 > v_2$, then $^1\mu_2 > 1$ and Sini>Sinr or i>r i.e., the refracted ray bends towards the normal. The medium 2 is said to be optically denser than medium 1. Hence a ray of light bends towards the normal as it refracts from a rarer medium into a denser medium.

(ii) If $v_1 < v_2$, then $^1\mu_2 < 1$ and Sini<Sinr or i<r i.e., he refracted ray bends away from the normal. The medium 2 is said to optically rarer than medium 1. Hence a ray of light bends away from the normal as it refracts from a denser medium into a rarer medium.

Physical significance of refractive index:

The refractive index of a medium gives the following two information:

(i) The value of refractive index gives information about the direction of bending of refracted ray.

It tells whether the ray will bend towards or away from the normal.

(ii) The refractive index of a medium is related to the speed of light. It is the ratio of the speed of light in vacuum to that in the given medium. For example, refractive index of glass is 3 /2. This indicates that the ratio of the speed of light in glass to that in vacuum is 2:3 or the speed of light in glass is two-third of its speed in vacuum.

3.5 *Practical applications of refraction of light: Real and apparent depths.*

It is on account of refraction of light that the apparent depth of an object placed in denser medium is less than the real depth. Fig. 3.4 shows a point object O placed at the bottom of a beaker filled with water. The rays OA and OB starting from O are refracted along AD and BC, respectively. These rays appear to diverge from point I.

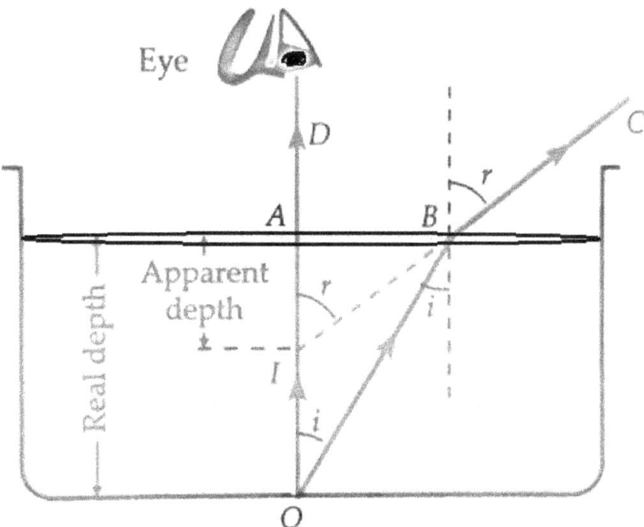

Fig. 3.4 Real and apparent depths.

So I is the virtual image of O. Clearly, the apparent depth AI is smaller than the real depth AO. That is why a water tank appears shallower or an object placed at the bottom appears to be raised.

From Snell's law, we have

$$^{a}\mu_{a} = \frac{Sin\,i}{Sin\,r} = \frac{Sin\angle AOB}{Sin\angle AIB} = \frac{AB/BO}{AB/BI} = \frac{BI}{BO}$$

$$3.6$$

As the size of the pupil is small, the ray BC will enter the eye only if B is close to A. Then

$$BI = AI$$
$$BO = AO$$
$$^{a}\mu_{a} = \frac{1}{^{a}\mu_{a}} = \frac{AO}{AI}$$

$$3.7$$

$$\text{Refractive Index} = \frac{Real\ Depth}{Apparent\ Depth}$$

$$Apparent\ Depth = \frac{Real\ Depth}{Refractive\ Index}$$

$$3.8$$

As the refractive index of any medium (other than vacuum) is greater than unity, so the apparent depth is less than the real depth.

Normal shift: The height through which an object appears to be raised in a denser medium is called normal shift. Clearly

Normal shift = Real depth - Apparent depth

$$d = AO - AI = AO - \frac{AO}{\mu}$$

$$d = AO\left(1 - \frac{1}{\mu}\right)$$

$$d = t\left(1 - \frac{1}{\mu}\right)$$

3.9

Clearly, the normal shift in the position of an object when seen through a denser medium depends on two factors:
1. The real depth of the object or the thickness (t) of the refracting medium.
2. The refractive index of the denser medium. The higher the value of μ greater is the apparent shift'd'.

How does the refraction of light affect the length of the day?

Apparent shift in the position of the sun at sunrise and sunset. Due to the atmospheric refraction, the sun is visible before actual sunrise and after actual sunset.

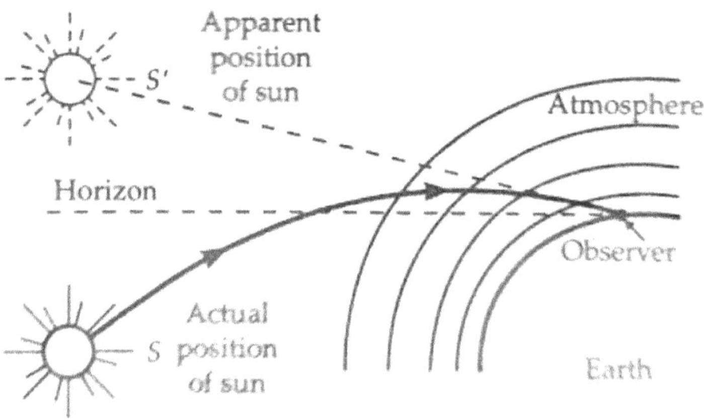

Fig. 3.5 Refraction effect at sunset and sunrise.

With altitude, the density and hence refractive index of air-layers decreases, the light rays starting from the sun S travel from rarer to denser layers. They bend more and more towards the normal. However, an observer sees an object in the direction of the rays reaching his eyes, so to an observer standing on the earth, the sun which is actually in a position S below the horizon, appears in the position S, above the horizon. The apparent shift in the direction of the sun is by about 0.59, Thus the sun appears to rise early by about 2 minutes and for the same reason, it appears to set late by about 2 minutes, This increases the length of the day by about 4 minutes.

3.6 Total Internal Reflection

If light passes from an optically denser medium to a rarer medium, then at the interface, the light is partly reflected back into the denser medium and partly refracted to the rarer medium. This reflection is called internal reflector. Under certain conditions, the whole of the incident light can be made to be reflected back into the denser medium. This gives rise to an interesting phenomenon called total internal reflection.

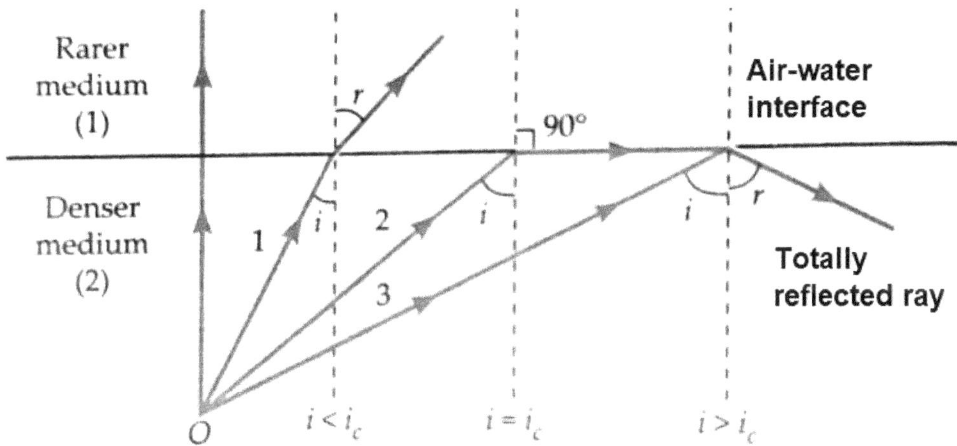

Fig. 3.6 Total internal reflection.

As shown in Fig. 3.6, when a ray of light (ray 1) travels at a small angle of incidence from a denser medium to a rarer medium, say from water to air, the refracted ray bends away from the normal so that the angle of refraction is greater than the angle of incidence. As the angle of incidence increases, the corresponding angle of refraction also increases. Then for a certain angle of incidence (ray 2), the angle of refraction becomes 90, ie., the refracted ray goes along the surface of separation.

The angle of incidence in the denser medium for which the angle of refraction in the rarer medium is

90° is called critical angle of the denser medium and is denoted by i.

If the angle of incidence is increased beyond 1, (ray 3), no light is refracted into the rarer medium since the angle of refraction cannot be greater than 90^0, but whole of it is reflected back into the denser medium in accordance with the laws of reflection. This phenomenon is known as total internal reflection.

The phenomenon in which a ray of light travelling at an angle of incidence greater than the critical angle from denser to a rarer medium is totally reflected back into the denser medium is called total internal reflection.

Necessary conditions for total internal reflection:

1. Light must travel from an optically denser to an optically rarer medium.

2. The angle of incidence in the denser medium must be greater than the critical angle for the two media.

Relation between critical angle and refractive index.

From Snell's law,

$$\frac{Sin i}{Sin r} = {^2\mu_1} = \frac{1}{{^1\mu_2}}$$

3.10

When i=i$_c$, r=90^0, therefore

$$\frac{Sin\,i_c}{Sin\,90^0} = \frac{1}{^1\mu_2}$$

$$^1\mu_2 = \frac{1}{Sin\,i_c}$$

3.11

If the rarer medium is air, then, μ1 =1 and μ2= μ (say) and we get

$$\mu = \frac{1}{Sin\,i_c}$$

3.12

Thus the refractive index of any medium is equal to the reciprocal of the sine of its critical angle.

3.7 *Applications of total internal reflection:*

The phenomenon of total internal reflection can be used to explain some effects observed in daily life and also it finds use in some optical devices as explained below:

1. Sparkling of diamond. The brilliancy of diamonds is due to total internal reflection. As the refractive index of diamond is very large, its critical angle is very small, about 24,4^0, The faces of diamond are so cut that the light entering the crystal suffers total is internal reflections repeatedly, and hence gets collected inside but it comes out through only a few faces, Hence the diamond sparkles when seen in the direction of emerging light.

2. Mirage. It is an optical illusion observed in deserts or F 0ver hot extended Surfaces like a coal-tarred road, due to which n traveller sees a shimmering pond of water some distance ahead of him and in which the surrounding objects like trees, etc, appear inverted.

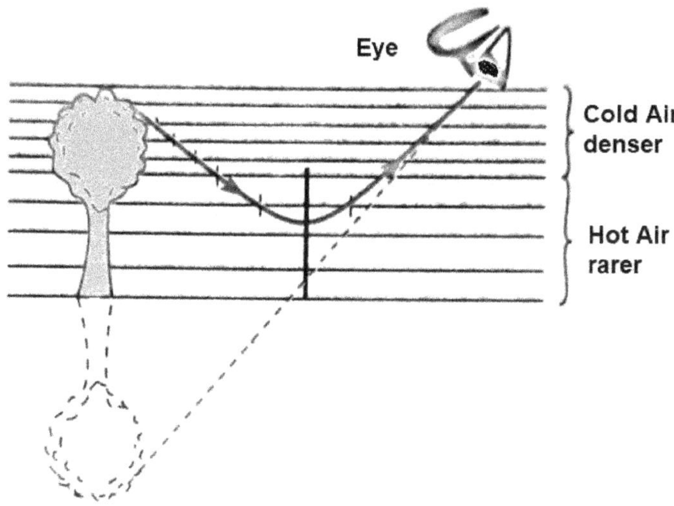

Fig. 3.7 Formation of mirage.

On a hot summer day, the surface of the earth becomes very hot. The layers of air near the earth are more heated than the higher ones. Hence the density and refractive index of air layers increase as we move high up. As the rays of light from a distant object like a tree travel towards the earth through layers of decreasing refractive index, they bend more and more away from the normal. A stage is reached when the angle of incidence becomes greater than the critical angle, the rays are totally reflected. These rays then move up through layers of increasing refractive index, and therefore undergo refraction in a direction opposite to that in the first case. These rays reach the observer's eyes and he sees an inverted image of the object, as if formed in a pond of water.

3.8 Optical fibres

These days we find in the market some decorative lamps provided with fine plastic fibres. At their one ends, the fibres are fixed over an electric lamp while their free ends form a fountain like structure. When the lamp is switched on, the light travels from the bottom of each fibre and appears at the tip of free end as a bright dot of light. The plastic fibres in these lamps are optical fibres. The working of optical fibres is based on the phenomenon of total internal reflection.

An optical fibre is a hair- thin long strand of quality glass or quartz Surrounded by a glass coating of slightly lower reflective index. It is used as a guided medium for transmitting an optical signal from one place to another.

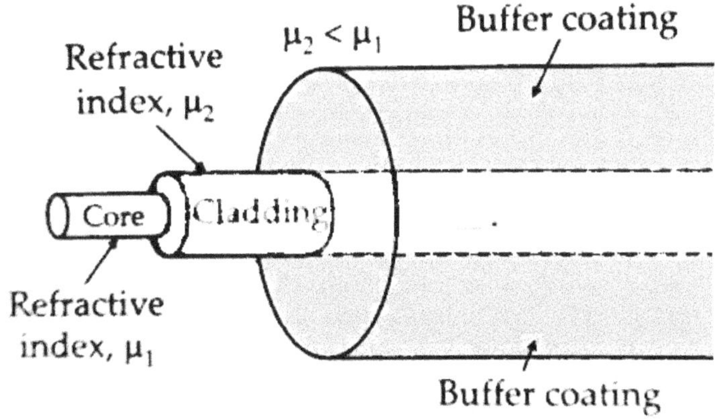

Fig 3.8 Optical Fibre

Construction: An optical fibre consists of three main parts:

(i) Core. The central cylindrical core is made of high quality glass/silica/plastic of refractive index, and has a diameter about 10 to 100 μm.

(ii) Cladding, The core is surrounded by a glass / plastic jacket of refractive index μ2<μ1. In a typical optical fibre, the refractive indices of core and cladding may be1.52 and 1.48 respectively.

(iii) Buffer coating. For providing safety and strength, the core cladding of optical fibres is enclosed in a plastic jacket.

Propagation of light through an optical fibre. As shown in Fig, 9.39(0), when light is incident on one end of the fibre at a small angle, it goes inside and suffers repeated total internal reflections because the angle of incidence is greater than the critical angle of the fibre material with respect to its outer coating, As there is no loss of intensity in total internal reflection, the light out coming beam is of as much intensity as the incident beam. Even if the fibre is bent, light easily travels through along the fibre.

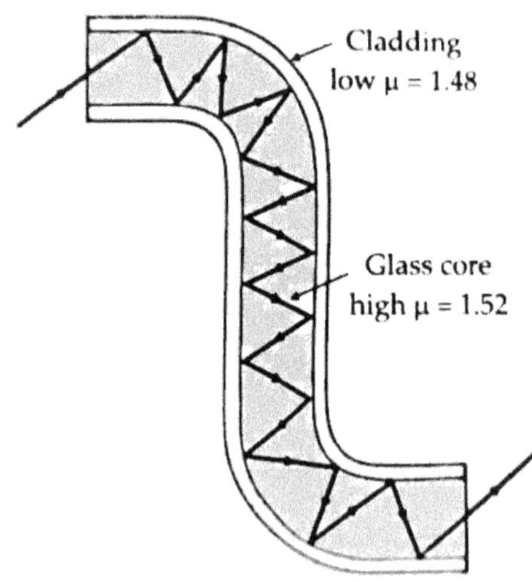

3.9 Propagation of light through an optical fibre

A bundle of optical fibres is called a light pipe. A single fibre cannot be used to see the complete image of an object. But, if the image is broken into a large number of fine dots and each portion of the image is seen through a separate fibre, the complete image can be seen. A light pipe can be used to transmit such an image accurately.

Applications of optical fibres. Some of the important applications are as follows:

1. As a light pipe, optical fibres are used in medical and optical examination, a light pipe is inserted into the Stomach through the mouth. Light transmitted through the outer layers of the light pipe is scattered by the various parts of stomach into the central portion of the light pipe to produce a final image with excellent details. The technique is called endoscopy.

2. They are used in transmitting and receiving electrical signals in telecommunication. The electrical signals are first converted to light by suitable transducers. Each fibre can transmit about 2000 telephone conversations without much loss of intensity.

3. They are used for transmitting optical signals and two dimensional pictures. 4. In the form of photometric sensors, they are used for measuring the blood flow in, the heart.

5. In the form of refractometers, they are used to measure refractive indices of liquids.

3.9 Spherical Lenses.

Most of us are familiar with lenses. As magnifying glasses, lenses have been in use for centuries. Lenses used in spectacles help us to read with comfort. Various optical instruments like camera, projector, microscope, telescopes, etc., cannot function without lenses.

A lens is a piece of a refracting medium bounded by two surfaces, at least one of which is a curved surface.

The commonly used lenses are the spherical lenses. These lenses have either both surfaces spherical or one spherical and the other a plane one. Lenses can be divided into two categories:

(i) Convex or converging lenses, and

(ii) Concave or diverging lenses.

(i) Convex or converging lens. It is thicker at the centre than at the edges. It converges a parallel beam of light on refraction through it. It has a real focus.

Types of convex lenses:

(a) Double convex or biconvex lens. In this lens, both surfaces are convex.

(b) Planoconcave lens. In this lens, one side is convex and the other is plane.

(c) Concavoconvex. In this lens, one side is convex and the other is concave.

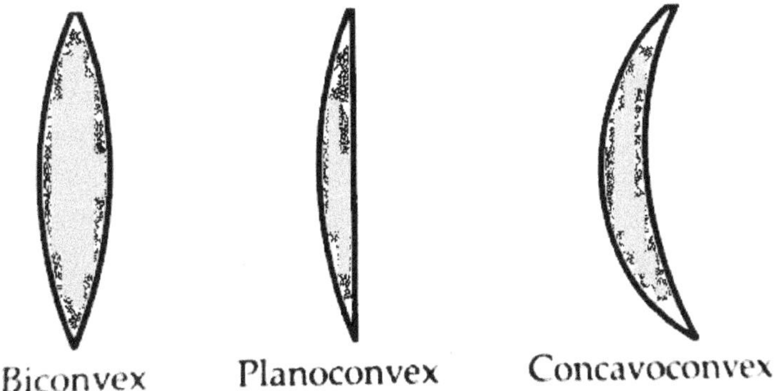

Fig 3.10 different types of convex lenses

(ii) Concave or diverging lens. It is thinner at the centre than at the edges. It diverges a parallel beam of light on refraction through it. It has a virtual focus.

Types of concave lenses:

(a) Double concave or biconcave lens. In this lens, both sides are concave,

(b) Planoconcave lens. In this lens, one side is plane and the other is concave.

(c) Convexoconcave lens. In this lens, one side is convex and the other is concave.

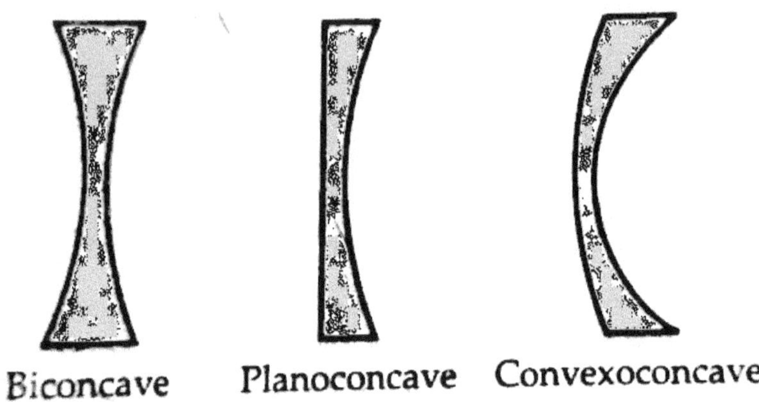

Fig 3.11 Different types of concave lens

3.10 Definitions in connection with spherical lenses:

(i) Centre of curvature (C). The centre of curvature of the surface of a lens is the centre of the sphere of which it forms a part. Because a lens has two surfaces, so it has two centres of curvature.

(ii) Radius of curvature (R). The radius of curvature of the surface of a lens is the radius of the sphere of which the Surface forms a part.

(iii) Principal axis (C_1C_2). It is the line passing through the two centres of curvature of the lens.

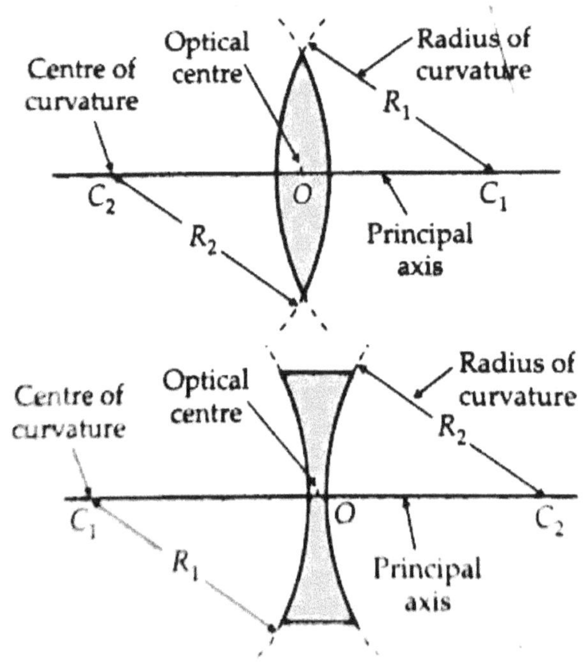

Fig. 3.12 Characteristics of convex and concave lenses.

(iv) Optical centre. If a ray of light is incident on a lens f such that after refraction through the lens the emergent ray is parallel to the incident ray, then the point at which the refracted ray intersects the principal axis is called the optical centre of the lens. In Fig. 3.13(a), O is the optical centre of the lens. It divides the thickness of the lens in the ratio of the radii of curvature of its two surfaces. Thus: If the radii of curvature of the two surfaces are equal, then the optical centre coincides with the geometric centre of the lens.

$$\frac{OP_1}{OP_2} = \frac{P_1C_1}{P_2C_2} = \frac{R_1}{R_2}$$

3.13

For the ray passing through the optical centre, the incident and emergent rays are parallel. However, the emergent ray suffers some lateral displacement relative to the incident ray. This lateral displacement decreases with the decrease in thickness of the lens.

Hence a ray passing through the optical centre of a thin lens does not suffer any lateral deviation, as shown in Figs. 3.13 (b) and (c).

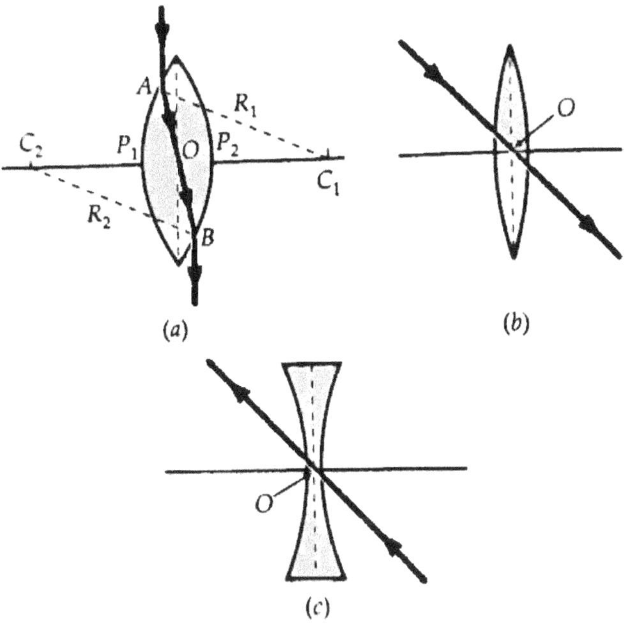

Fig 3.13 Optical Centre

(v) Principal foci and focal length:

First principal focus. It is a fixed point on the principal axis such that rays starting from this point (in convex lens)

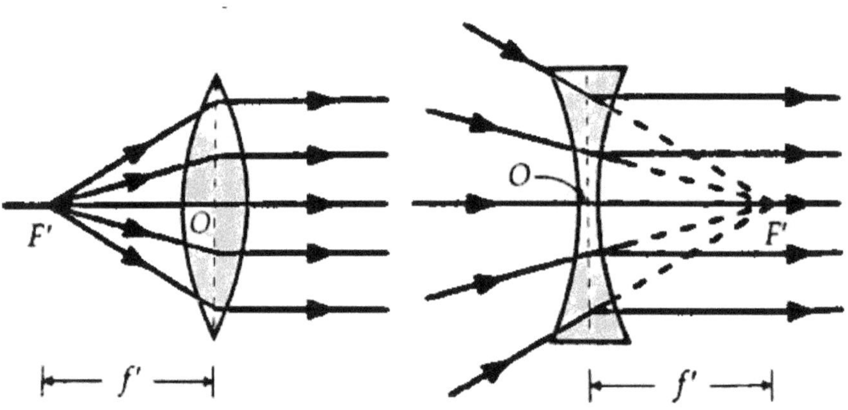

Fig 3.14 First principal focus and first focal length.

or appearing to go towards this point (in concave lens), after refraction through the lens, become parallel to the principal axis. It is represented by F or F'. The plane passing through this point and perpendicular to the principal axis is called the first focal plane. The distance between first principal focus and the optical centre is called the first focal length. It is denoted by f, or f'.

Second principal focus. It is a fixed point on the principal axis such that the light rays incident parallel to the principal axis, after refraction through the lens, either converge to this point (in convex lens) or appear to diverge from this point (in concave lens). The plane passing through this point and perpendicular to principal axis is called the second focal plane. The distance between the second principal focus and the optical centre is called the second focal length. It is denoted by f, or f.

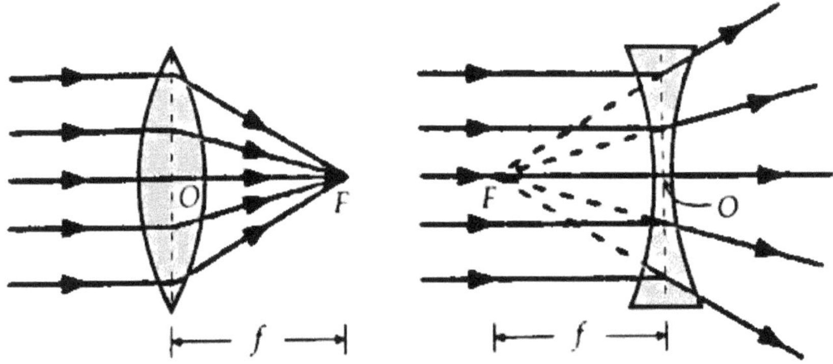

Fig 3.15 Second principal focus and first focal length.

Generally, the focal length of a lens refers to its second focal length. It is obvious from the above figures that the foci of a convex lens are real and those of a concave lens are virtual. Thus the focal length of a convex lens is taken positive and the focal length of a concave lens is taken negative.

If the medium on both sides of a lens is same, then the numerical values of the first and second focal lengths are equal. Thus f=f'.

(vi) Aperture. It is the diameter of the circular boundary of the lens.

New Cartesian sign convention for spherical lenses.

1. All distances are measured from the optical centre of the lens.

2. The distances measured in the same direction as the incident light are taken positive.

3. The distances measured in the direction opposite to the direction of the incident light are taken negative.

4. Heights measured upwards and perpendicular to the principal axis are taken positive.

5. Heights measured downwards and perpendicular to the principal axis are taken negative.

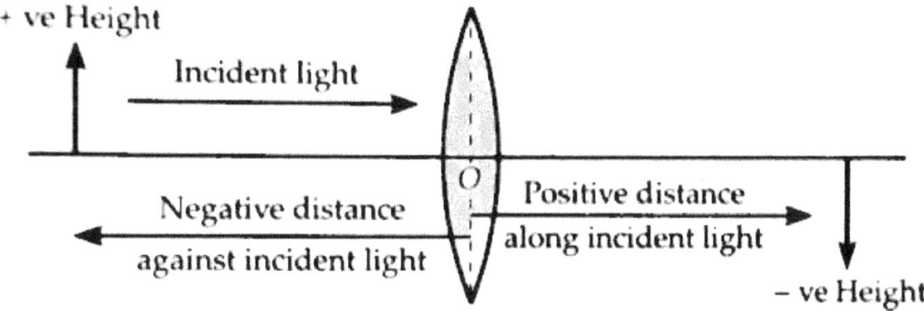

Fig. 3.16 New Cartesian sign convention for a spherical lens.

Consequences of the sign convention:

1. The focal length of a converging lens is positive and that of a diverging lens is negative.

2. Object distance is always negative.

3. The distance of real image is positive and that of virtual image is negative.

4. The object height h, is always positive. Height h1, of virtual erect image is positive and that of real inverted image is negative.

5. The linear magnification m= h2/h1, is positive for a virtual image and negative for a real image.

Before deriving formulae for spherical lenses, we first consider refraction by a single spherical surface.

3.11 Rules for drawing images formed by spherical lenses.

The position of the image formed by any spherical lens can be found by considering any two of the following rays of light coming from a point on the object.

(i) A ray from the object parallel to the principal axis after refraction passes through the second principal focus F, [in a convex lens, as shown in Fig. 3.17(a)] Or appears to diverge [in a concave lens, as shown in Fig. 3.17(b)] from the first principal focus F1

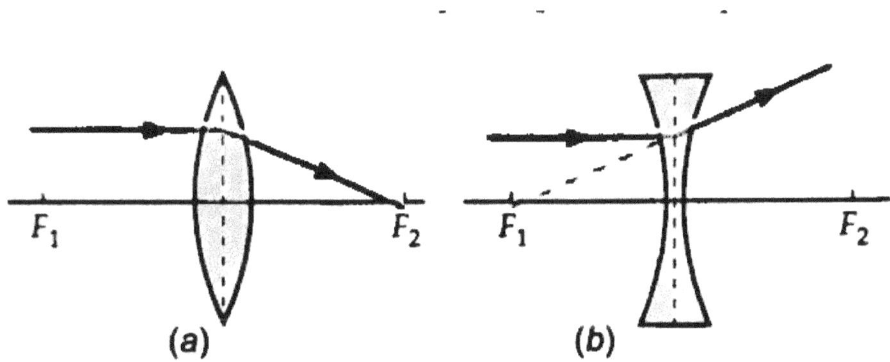

Fig. 3.17 Path of ray incident parallel to the principal axis of (a) convex lens (b) concave lens.

(ii) A ray of light passing through the first principal focus in a convex lens, as shown in Fig. 3.18(a)] or appearing to meet at it in a concave lens, as shown in Fig. 3.18(b)] emerges parallel to the principal axis after refraction.

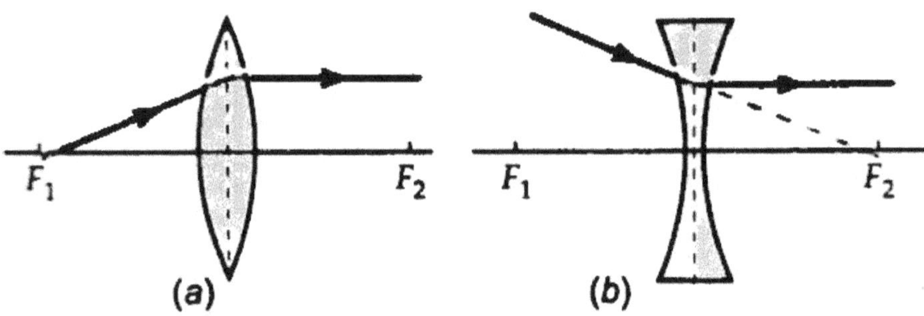

Fig, 3.18 Path of a ray passing through focus of (a) convex lens (b) concave lens.

(iii) A ray of light, passing through the optical centre of the lens, emerges without any deviation after refraction, as shown in Figs. 3.19(a) and (b).

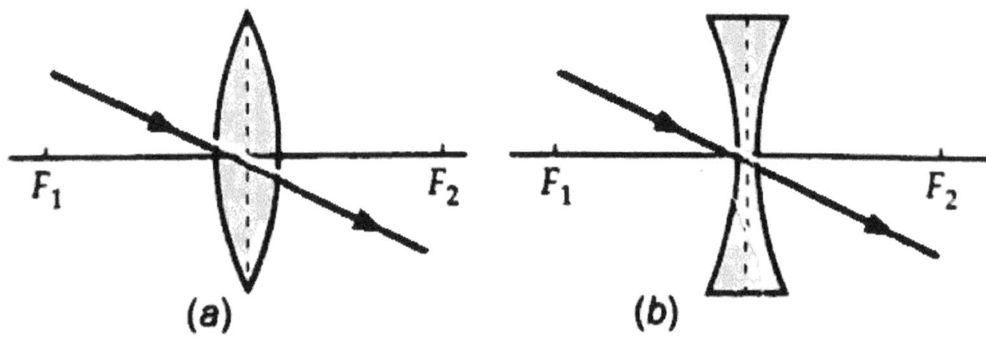

Fig 3.19 Path of a ray passing through the optical centre (a) convex lens (b) concave lens.

Formation of image for different position of object:
a) If the object is placed beyond 2F:

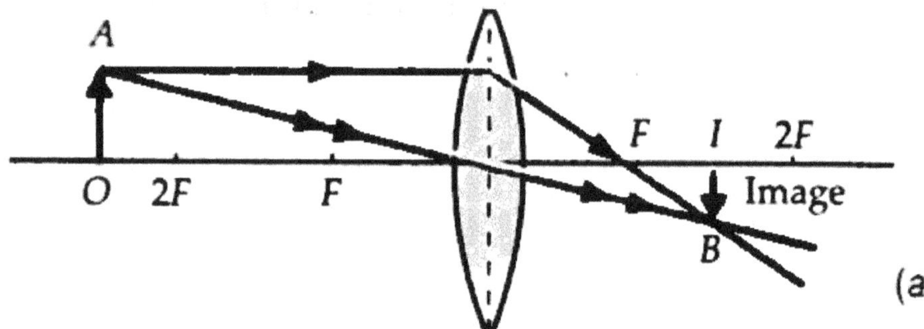

Fig 3.20 Image for an object placed beyond 2F

b) If the object is place at 2F:

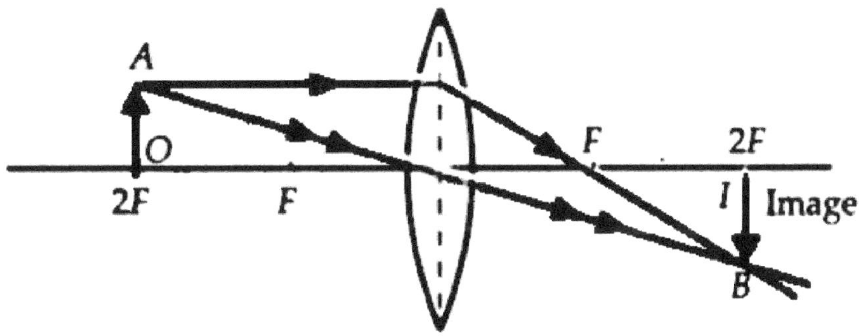

Fig 3.21 Image for an object placed at 2F

c) If the object is placed between 2F and F:

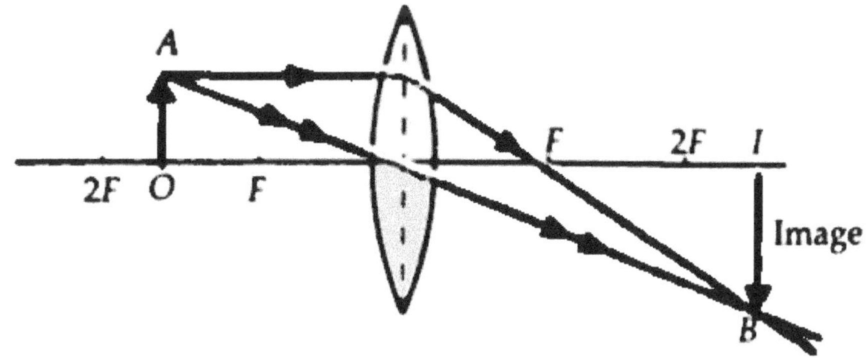

Fig 3.22 Image for an object placed between 2F and F

d) If the object is placed between F and O:

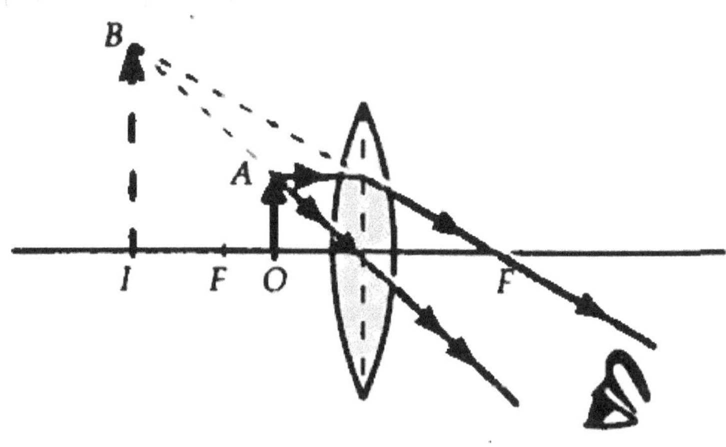

Fig 3.23 Image for an object placed between F and O

e) If the object is placed in any position:

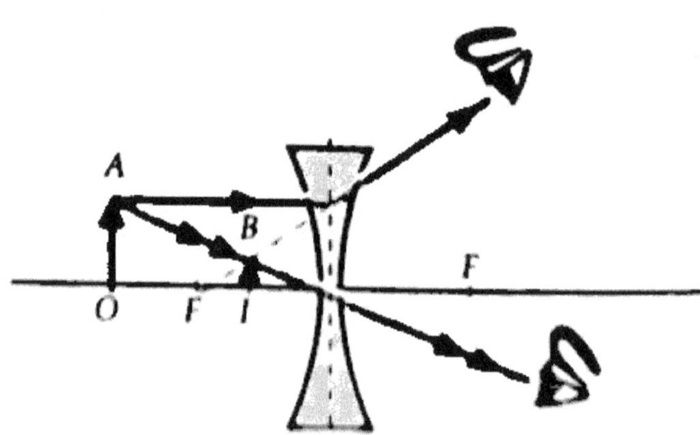

Fig 3.24 Image for an object placed in any position

3.12 Thin lens formula:

Thin lens formula is a mathematical relation between the object distance u, image distance v and focal length f of a spherical lens. This relation is:

$$\frac{1}{v} - \frac{1}{u} = \frac{1}{f}$$

3.14

In words, we can say that

$$\frac{1}{\text{Image distance}} - \frac{1}{\text{Object distance}} = \frac{1}{\text{Focal Length}}$$

3.15

This formula is valid for both convex and concave lenses for both real and virtual images.

Derivation of thin lens formula for a convex lens:

Assumptions used in the derivation of lens formula:

(i) The lens used is thin.

(ii) The aperture of the lens is small.

(iii) The incident and refracted rays make small angles with the principal axis.

(iv) The object is a small object placed on the principal axis.

When it forms a real image. As shown in Fig. 3.25, consider an object AB placed perpendicular to the principal axis of a thin convex lens between its F' and C. A real, inverted and magnified image A' B is formed beyond C on the other side of the lens.

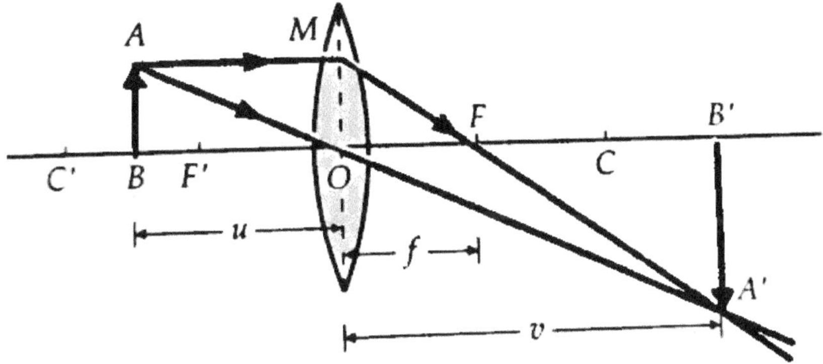

Fig. 3.25 Real image formed by a convex lens.

Triangle A'B'O and Triangle ABO are similar,

$$\frac{A'B'}{AB} = \frac{OB'}{BO}$$

3.16

Also Triangle A'B'F and Triangle MOF are similar,

$$\frac{A'B'}{MO} = \frac{FB'}{OF}$$

3.17

But MO = AB,

$$\frac{A'B'}{AB} = \frac{FB'}{OF}$$

3.18

From (1) and (2), we get

$$\frac{OB'}{BO} = \frac{FB'}{OF} = \frac{OB' - OF}{OF}$$

3.19

Using new Cartesian sign convention, we get
Object distance, BO =- u
Image distance, OB' =+ U
Focal length, OF =+ f

$$\frac{v}{-u} = \frac{v-f}{f}$$

3.20

Dividing both sides by uvf, we get

$$\frac{1}{f} = \frac{1}{v} - \frac{1}{u}$$

3.21

This proves the lens formula for a convex lens when it forms a real image.

3.13 *Linear magnification*

The linear magnification produced by a lens is defined as the ratio of the size of the image formed by the lens to the size of the object. It is denoted by m. Thus
m= (Size of image)/ (Size of object)=h2/h1
For Convex lens:
Earlier Fig. 3.25 shows a ray diagram for the formation of image A' B of a finite object AB by a convex lens.
Now triangle AOB ~Triangle A'OB'

$$\frac{A'B'}{AB} = \frac{OB'}{OB}$$

3.22

Applying the new Cartesian sign convention, we get
(Downward image height) A'B'= -h_2, (Upward object height) AB= + h_1
(Image distance on left) OB= -u, (Image distance on right) OB'= +v

$$\frac{-h_2}{+h_1} = \frac{+v}{-u} \quad \text{or} \quad \frac{h_2}{h_1} = \frac{v}{u}$$

3.23

Magnification

$$m = \frac{h_2}{h_1} = \frac{v}{u}$$

3.24

For Concave lens magnification is also

$$m = \frac{h_2}{h_1} = \frac{v}{u}$$

3.14 *Power of a lens:*

The power of a lens is a measure of the degree of convergence or divergence of the light rays falling on it. As shown in Fig. 3.26, a convex lens of shorter focal length bends light rays towards the principal axis through a larger angle, by focussing them closer to the optical centre. Hence smaller the focal length of a lens, more is ability to bend light rays and greater is its power.

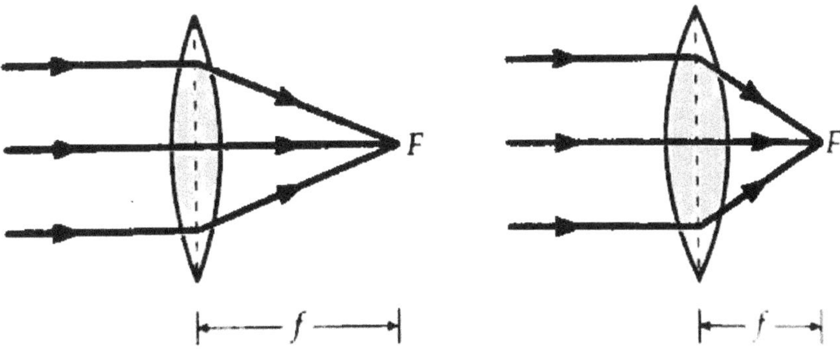

Fig. 3.26 (a) Large f, small bending power, (b) Small f, large bending power.

The power of a lens is defined as the tangent of the angle by which it converges or diverges a beam of light falling at unit distance from the optical centre.

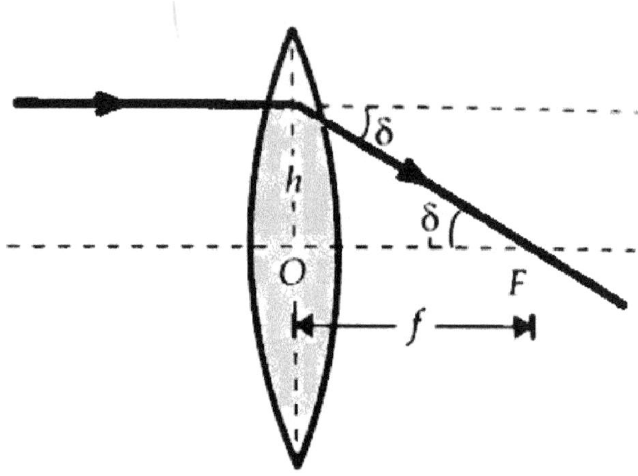

Fig 3.27 Power of lens

In Fig. 3.27, a beam of light is incident at distance h from the optical centre O of a convex lens of focal length f. It converges the beam by angle &

$$\tan \delta = \frac{h}{f}$$

$$if \ h=1, \ then \ \tan \delta = \frac{1}{f}$$

$$or \ P = \frac{1}{f}$$

3.25

Thus the power of a lens may also be defined as the reciprocal of its focal length.

SI unit of power: The SI unit of power is dioptre, denoted by D If f=1m, then One dioptre is the power of a lens whose principal focal F length is l metre.

The focal length of a converging lens is positive and that of a diverging lens is negative. Thus, the power of t converging lens is positive and that of a diverging lens is negative. We can measure the power of a lens directly by a device called dioptremeter. Thus, when an optician prescribes a corrective lens of power + 2.5 D,

The required lens is a convex lens of focal length, f =1/(+ 2.5 D) =+0.40 m =+ 40 cm.

Similarly, a power of -4.0 D means a concave lens of focal length -25 cm.

By using lens maker's formula, the power of a lens can be expressed in terms of its refractive index u and radii of curvature R_1 and R_2 as follows:

$$P = \frac{1}{f} = (\mu - 1)\left[\frac{1}{R_1} - \frac{1}{R_2}\right]$$

3.26

As the power of a lens is reciprocal of its focal length, so it characterises the focal properties of the lens, such as nature, size and position of image, etc.

3.15 Optical instruments:

Optical instruments are the devices which make use of mirrors, lenses and prisms and are primarily used to extend the range of vision of human eye. For example, microscopes are used for viewing tiny objects clearly while telescopes are used to see distant objects clearly.

Essential features of an optical instrument. The design of an optical instrument must meet the following two requirements:

1. High magnification. Magnification is the ratio of the size of the final image to the size of the object. An optical instrument with high magnification makes viewing more clear and comfortable, by increasing the size of the image.

2. Adequate resolution. The resolution of an optical instrument is its ability to resolve the images of two closely spaced objects so that they can be seen separately. An optical instrument with high resolution reveals the finer details of the objects.

Simple microscope:

A simple microscope or a magnifying glass is just a convex lens of short focal length, held close to the eye.

Working principle: When the final image is formed at the least distance of distinct vision. When an object AB is placed between the focus F and optical centre O of a convex lens; a virtual, erect and magnified image AB is formed on the same side of the lens as the object. Since a normal eye can see an object clearly at the least distance of distinct vision D (=25 cm), the position of the lens is so adjusted that the final image is formed at the distance D from the lens, as shown in Fig. 3.28.

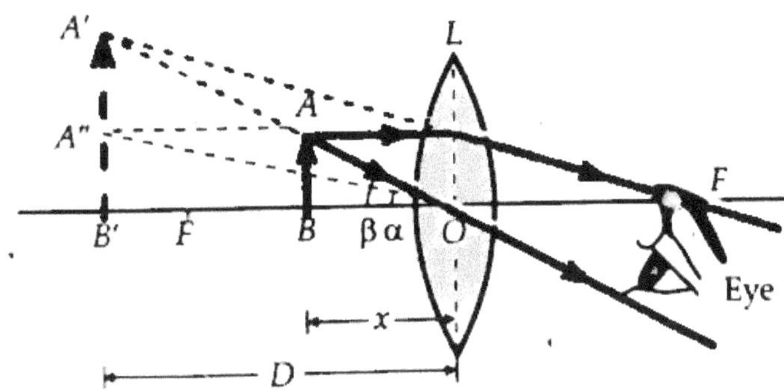

Fig. 3.28 Simple microscope with the eye focussed at the near point.

Magnifying power: The magnifying power of a simple microscope is defined as the ratio of the angles subtended by the image and the object at the eye, when both are at the least distance of distinct vision from the eye. Thus,

$$\text{Magnifying power} = \frac{\text{Angle subtended by the image at the least distance of distinct vision}}{\text{Angle subtended by the object at the least distance of distinct vision}}$$

3.27

$$m = 1 + \frac{D}{f}$$

3.28

Thus shorter the focal length of the convex lens, the greater is its magnifying power.

Working principle: When the final image is formed at infinity. When we see an image at the near point, it causes some strain in the eye. Often the object is placed at the focus of the convex lens, so that parallel rays enter the eye, as shown in Fig. 3.29 (a). The image is formed at infinity, which is more suitable and comfortable for viewing by the relaxed eye.

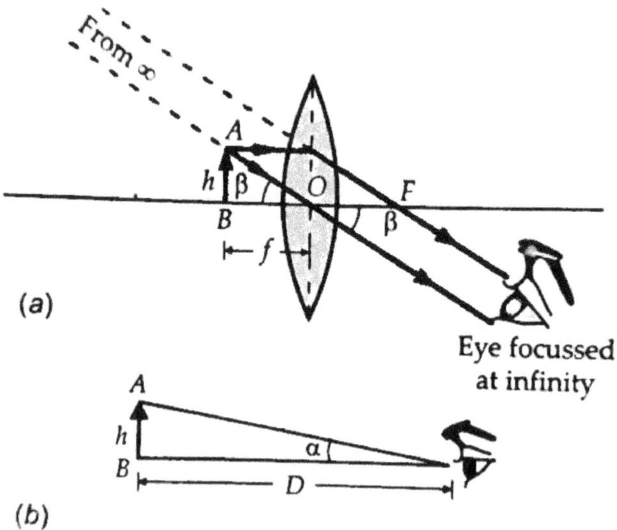

Fig. 3.29 Image is formed at infinity

Uses of simple microscopes:

1, Watch makers and jewellers use a magnifying glass for having a magnified view of the small parts of watches and the fine jewellery work.

2. In magnifying the printed letters in a book, textures of fibres or threads of a cloth, engravings, details of stamp, etc.

3. Magnifying glass is used in science laboratories for reading vernier scales, etc.

Compound microscope:

A compound microscope is an optical device used to see magnified images of tiny objects. A good quality compound microscope can produce magnification of the order of 1000.

Construction. It consists of two convex lenses of short focal length, arranged co-axially at the ends of too sliding metal tubes.

1. Objective. It is a convex lens of very short focal length f_0 and small aperture. It is positioned near the object to be magnified.

2. Eyepiece or ocular. It is a convex lens of comparatively larger focal length fe and larger aperture than the objective (fe > f_0) It is positioned near the eye for viewing the final image.

The distance between the two lenses can be varied by using rack and pinion arrangement.

Working. (a) When the final image is formed at the least distance of distinct vision. The object AB to be viewed is placed at distance u slightly larger than the focal length f_0 of the objective O. The objective forms a real, inverted and magnified image A B, of the object AB on the other side of the lens O, as shown in Fig. 3.30. The separation between the objective O and the eyepiece E, is so adjusted that the image A B' lies within the focal length fe of the eyepiece. The image AB acts as an object for the eyepiece which essentially acts like a simple microscope. The eyepiece E forms a virtual and magnified final image A" B' of the object AB. Clearly, the final image A' B' is inverted with respect to the object AB

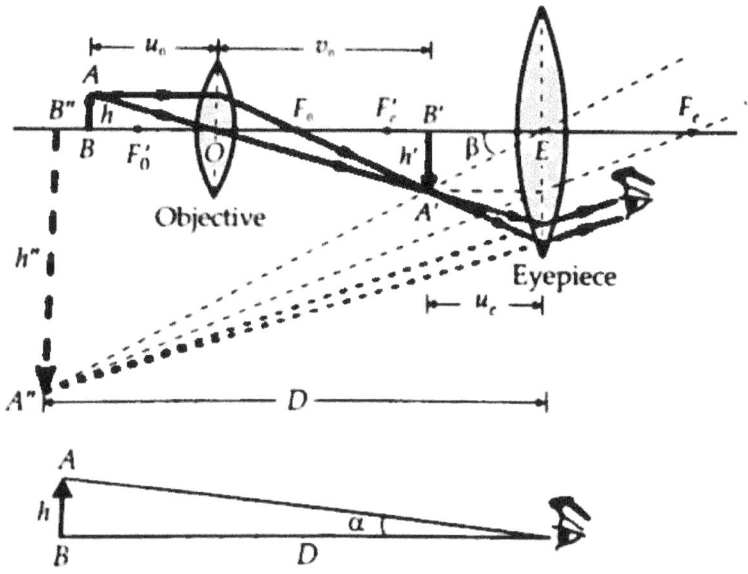

Fig. 3.30 Compound Microscope, final image at D.

Magnifying power. The magnifying power of a compound microscope is defined as the ratio of the angle subtended at the eye by the final virtual image to the angle subtended at the eye by the object, when both are at the least distance of distinct vision from the eye.

Different types of telescope:

Broadly, the telescopes can be divided into two categories

1. Refracting telescopes. These make use of lenses to view distant objects. These are of two types:

(a) Astronomical telescope. It is used to see heavenly objects like the sun, stars, planets, etc. The final image formed is inverted one which is immaterial in the case of heavenly bodies because of their round shape.

(b) Terrestrial telescope. It is used to see distant objects on the surface of the earth. The final image formed is erect one. This is an essential condition of viewing the objects on earth's surface correctly.

2. Reflecting telescopes. These make use of converging mirrors to view the distant objects. For example, Newtonian and Cassegrain telescopes.

Astronomical telescope:

It is a refracting type telescope used to see heavenly bodies like stars, planets, satellites, etc.

Construction. It consists of two converging lenses mounted co-axially at the outer ends of two sliding tubes.

1. Objective. It is a convex lens of large focal length and a much larger aperture. It faces the distant object. In order to form bright image of the distant objects, the aperture of the objective is taken large so that it can gather sufficient light from the distant objects.

2. Eyepiece. It is a convex lens of small focal length and small aperture. It faces the eye. The aperture of the eyepiece is taken small so that whole light of the telescope may enter the eye for distinct vision.

Working. (a) When the final image is formed at the least distance of distinct vision. As shown in Fig.3.31, the parallel beam of light coming from the distant object falls on the objective at some angle a. The objective focusses the beam in its focal plane and forms a real, inverted and diminished image A B. This image AB acts as an object for the eyepiece. The distance of the eyepiece is so adjusted that the image AB lies within its focal length. The eyepiece magnifies this image so that final image A" B" is magnified and inverted with respect to the object. The final image is distinctly by the eye at the least distance distinct vision.

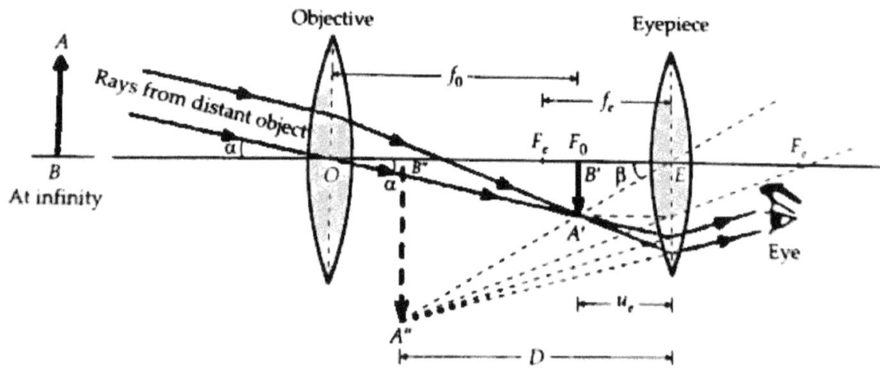

Fig 3.31 Astronomical Telescope

Magnifying power. The magnifying power of a telescope is defined as the ratio of the angle subtended at the eye by the final image formed at the least distance of distinct vision to the angle subtended at the eye y the object at infinity, when seen directly.

$$m = -\frac{f_0}{f_e}\left(1+\frac{f_e}{D}\right)$$

3.29

Magnifying Power in normal adjustment is

$$m = -\frac{f_0}{f_e}$$

3.30

3.16 Interference of light:

Thomas Young, in 1802, demonstrated the concept of interference of light by using, a light source and a double slit. The light was allowed to fall on a pinhole, S from which the spherical wavefronts are made to be incident on two pinhole S1 and S2. A few coloured bright and dark bands are observed on the screen PQ kept at a certain distance from the two pinholes (figure 3.32). Later young replaced white light by monochromatic source of light and the pinholes by narrow slits.

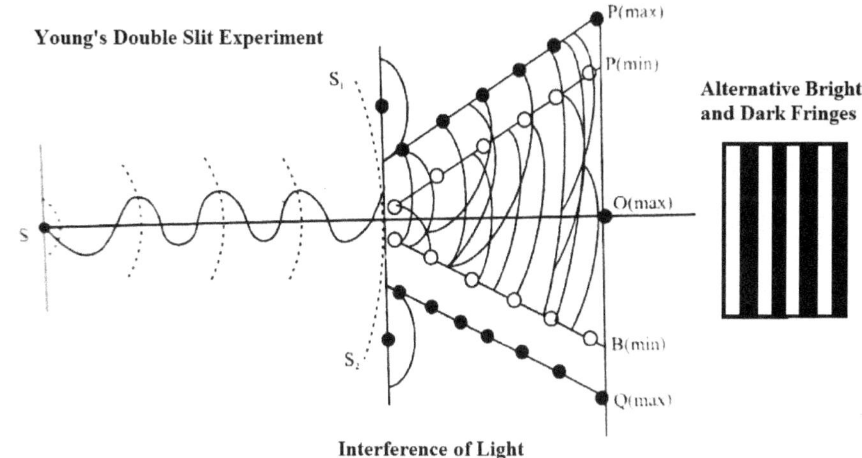

Figure 3.32: Young's Double-slit experiment

Wave fronts and their superposition

Point O on the screen is equidistant from the sources S, and S, and hence the path difference between the light waves reaching O from S, and S, is zero. So the point O will be the location of maximum intensity. At the point A or B on the screen the path difference between the two waves emerging from the slits S, and S, and meeting at A or B is /2 and as such the intensity at those points is the minimum. At the points P or Q on the screen the path difference between the two waves in and the intensity of light is maximum at these points.

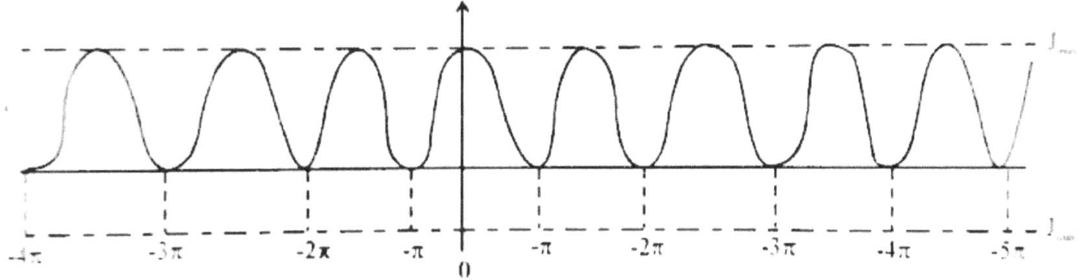

Fig 3.33 Intensity pattern for interference of light

When electrical waves from two sources overlap at a point in space, the combined wave intensity at that point can be greater or less than the intensity of either of the two waves. This effect is known as interference. The interference is constructive, when the net intensity is greater than the individual intensities and destructive, when the net intensity is less than the individual intensities. Depending on the relative phase of the two waves, the interference may either be constructive or destructive.

Although any number of waves can in principle interfere, the interference of only two waves is considered here. It is assumed that the sources emit wave at a single wavelength and the phase relationship between the two waves remains constant independent of time. Such waves are said to be "Coherent." When Coherent' waves interfere, the intensity of the combined wave at any point in space does not change with time. The coherence is a necessary condition for interference to occur and it is explained below:

Two light sources emitting waves of same frequency having nearly same amplitude with a constant phase difference are called coherent sources. Two different light sources not in general be made coherent, because the emission of light by the atoms of one source is independent of that of the other. The crests and troughs of the waves from the two sources do not maintain a definite phase relationship and so these waves are said to be incoherent.

The interference experiment can be carried out with light. To carry out this experiment it is necessary to divide the light from a single source into two components and to treat each components as if it were emitted from an independent source of light. The modification in this distribution of light energy due to superposition of two or more waves is called interference.

Coherent sources can be produced from a single source by two methods: (i) division of wave front and (ii) division of amplitude.

(i) Division of wave front: In the first method, the interfering waves are produced from single wave to maintain a constant phase relationship between the waves. The light from a single source is allowed to divided be incident on two closely spaced holes or apertures so that the single light be into two beams after emitting from the apertures and neighbouring parts of the wave front are separated. These separated beams superimpose to produce interference. The method of division of wave front is applied in young's experiment, Lloyd's single mirror and Fresnel Biprism experiment.

(ii) Division of amplitude: In the second method known as division of amplitude, a beam is divided at two or reflecting surfaces such as in this films or semi-transparent mirror and the reflected beams are separated and superimposed to produce interference effect. This method is applied Newton's rings, Michelson interferometer and thin films.

Interference of light and principle of superposition of light waves:

Interference is the property of light or any electromagnetic wave by virtue of which it produces alternate bright and dark bands or fringes due to superposition of two monochromatic light waves of same wavelengths and nearly same or same amplitude which maintain a constant phase difference while propagating in the same direction.

The principle of superposition of light waves may be stated as follows:

When two or more light waves travel simultaneously in a medium in the same direction and meet at a point then the resultant displacement at that particular point is obtained from the algebraic sum of the displacements of individual waves.

Conditions for sustained interference:

1. The interference pattern in which the position of maximum and minimum intensity of light remain fixed along the screen is called sustained interference.
2. The following conditions are to be satisfied for obtaining sustained interference:
3. The two sources must be coherent, i.e. the sources should emit waves in the same phase or they should maintain a constant phase difference between them.
4. The sources should emit light of same wavelength and same or nearly same amplitude.
5. The sources should be narrow and close to each other to observe distinct fringes.
6. The two lights must be in the same state of polarisation.
7. The two waves must propagate along the same direction in order to be superimposed.

Coherence

If a fixed and predictable phase difference between several waves travelling in a particular direction be maintained, then we say the motion is coordinated or coherent. The corresponding waves are called coherent waves and sources emitting them are called coherent source. Coherence effects are mainly of two types: (1) temporal coherence and (2) spatial coherence.

Temporal coherence:

If the phase difference at a single point in the bundle of light waves propagating in space, at the beginning and end of a fixed time interval does not change with time then the waves are said to have temporal coherence.

Spatial Coherence:

The continuity and uniformity of a wave in a direction perpendicular to the direction of propagation refers to spatial coherence the wave is said to have spatial coherence if the phase difference for any two fixed points in a plane normal to the wave propagation does not vary with time. The degree of contrast of the bright and dark interference fringes is a measure of the degree of spatial coherence of the source emitting the waves. Spatial coherence is better if the constant is higher.

3.17 Diffraction of light:

Like sound wave, light wave also suffers bending round the sharp edge of an obstacle if the dimension of the obstacle is comparable with the wavelength of the light wave. The phenomenon of bending of light waves around obstacles or apparatus of dimension comparable with the wavelength of light leading to spreading of light beam into the geometrical shadow of the object is called diffraction.

Classification of Diffraction

Diffraction phenomenon can be classified into two main categories i.e., (i)) Fresnel's diffraction and (ii) Fraunhofer's diffraction. In Fresnel's diffraction, either the source of light or the screen or both are at finite distances from the diffraction aperture. The wave front in this case is either spherical or cylindrical. In Fraunhofer's diffraction both the source of light and the screen are effectively at infinite distances from the diffracting aperture and the wavefront is plane.

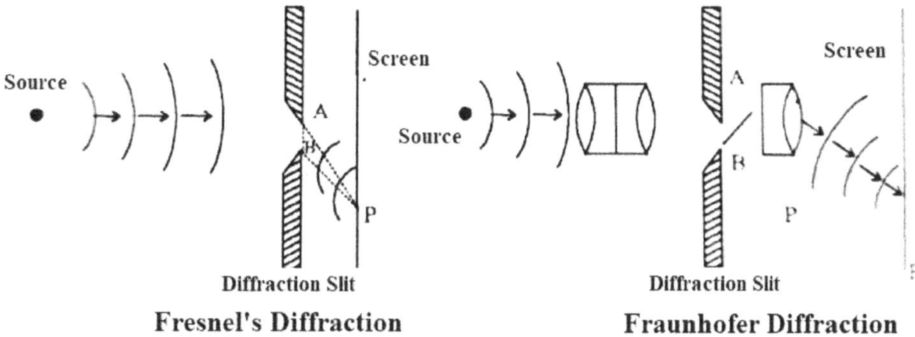

Fg: 3.34 Fresnel's diffraction and Fraunhofer diffraction

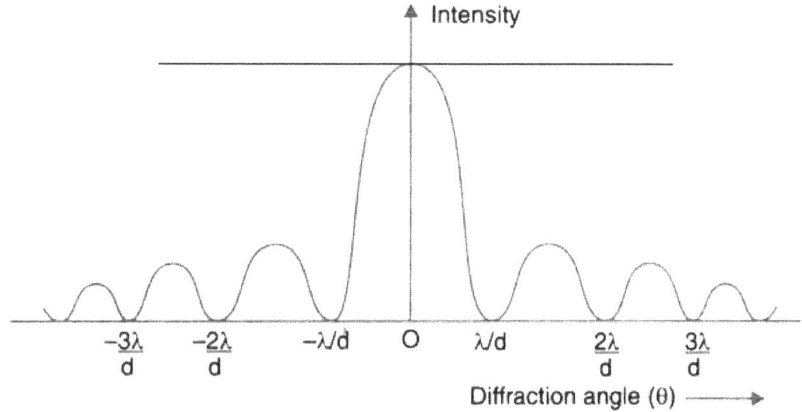

Fig 3.35 Intensity pattern for diffraction of light

Comparison of Fresnel's diffraction and Frunhofer's diffraction:

Fresnel's diffraction	Fraunhofer's diffraction
The distances of the source and the screen or both from the diffracting elements are finite.	The distances of the source and the screen or both from the diffracting elements are effectively infinite.
In the plane of the aperture the phase of the secondary wavelets are is not the same at all points.	The secondary wavelets are in same phase at every point in the plane of the aperture.
The wave fronts are either spherical or cylindrical.	The wave fronts are plane.

Comparison of interference and diffraction:

Interference	Diffraction
Interference is the result of interaction of light coming from two different wave fronts originating from the same source.	Diffraction pattern is the result of interaction of light coming from different part of same wave front.
The width of interference fringes may or may not be same.	The diffraction fringes are never of equal width.
All the bright fringes have the same intensity.	The intensity of the bright fringes usually decreases with increases of the order number.
All the dark fringes have zero intensity.	The intensity of dark fringes may not be zero.
Intensity distribution of interference pattern is uniform.	Intensity distribution of diffraction pattern is non-uniform.

Enter Caption

3.18 Numerical Problem and Solutions

1. A ray of light of frequency 15x10^{14} Hz is passed through a liquid. The wavelength of light measured inside the liquid is found to be 600 × 10^{-9} m Calculate the refractive index of the liquid.

Solution-

Here $v=15 \times 10^{14}$ Hz, $\lambda= 600 \times 10^{-9}$ m, $c=3 \times 10^{8}$ m/s

Refractive index of the liquid,

$$\mu = \frac{c}{v} = \frac{c}{\upsilon\lambda}$$

$$\mu = \frac{3\times10^8}{15\times10^{14}\times600\times10^{-9}} = 0.33$$

2. A light of wavelength 6000 Å in air, enters a medium with refractive index 2. What will be the frequency and wavelength of light in that medium?

Solution-

In air λ =6000 Ä=6x 10^{-7} m, c=3x 10^8 m/s

Refractive index of the medium, μ =2

When light travels from air to the refracting medium, its frequency remains unchanged.

$$\upsilon' = \upsilon = \frac{c}{\lambda}$$

$$\upsilon = \frac{3\times10^8}{6\times10^{-7}} = 5\times10^{14}\,Hz$$

Wavelength of light in the medium,

$$\lambda' = \frac{\lambda}{\mu}$$

$$\lambda' = \frac{6000}{2} = 3000\,\overset{\circ}{A}$$

3. The refractive index of glass is 1.5 and that of water is 1.3. If the speed of light in water is 2.45 x 10^8 ms^{-1}, what is the speed of light in glass?

Solution-

$$^a\mu_g = \frac{c}{\upsilon_g} = 1.5$$

$$^a\mu_w = \frac{c}{\upsilon_w} = 1.3$$

$$\frac{c}{\upsilon_w}\times\frac{\upsilon_g}{c} = \frac{1.3}{1.5}$$

$$\upsilon_g = \frac{1.3}{1.5}\times\upsilon_w = \frac{1.3}{1.5}\times 2.45\times10^8 = 2.12\times10^8\,m/s$$

4. Find the value of critical angle for a material of refractive index√3

Solution-

Here

$$\mu = \sqrt{3}$$

$$Sin i_c = \frac{1}{\mu} = \frac{1}{\sqrt{3}} = 0.58$$

$$Critical\ angle\ i_c = 35.3^0$$

5. Calculate the speed of light in a medium whose critical angle is 60°.

Solution-

Here i_c=60°

$$\mu = \frac{c}{v} = \frac{1}{Sin i_c}$$

$$v = c \times Sin i_c = 3 \times 10^8 \times Sin60^0$$

$$v = 2.6 \times 10^8\ m/s$$

6. A glass slab is immersed in water Find the critical angle at glass-water interface. Given.

$$^a\mu_g = 1.5\ \text{and}\ ^a\mu_w = 1.3$$

Solution-

$$\frac{Sin i}{Sin r} = \frac{\mu_w}{\mu_g}$$

$$\frac{Sin i_c}{Sin90^0} = \frac{1.33}{1.5}$$

$$Sin i_c = 0.8867$$

$$i_c = 62^0 28'$$

7. An object is placed at a certain distance from a convex lens of focal length 20 cm. Find the distance of the object if the image obtained is magnified 4 times.

Solution-

f = 20cm, m = 4, u =?

m = v/u = 4 or v = 4u

The lens equation is

1/f = 1/v − 1/u

1/f = 1/4u – 1/u

1/f = -3/4u

u = -3f / 4 = − 3 x20 / 4

u = − 15 cm

8. Two lenses with powers; 2D & -4D are kept together. What is the effective focal length of the combination?

Solution-

Effective power P=P1+P2

P=2D+(-4D)= -2D

Hence f=-1/2x100=-50 cm.

3.19 Objective Type questions with solution

1. Focal length of plane mirror is

   a. At infinity b. Zero c. Negative d. None of these

   Answer a

   2. Image formed by plane mirror is

   a. Real and erect b. Real and inverted c. Virtual and erect d. Virtual and inverted

   Answer c

   3. A concave mirror gives real, inverted and same size image if the object is placed

   a. At F b. At infinity c. At C d. beyond C

   Answer c

   4. Power of the lens is -40, its focal length is

   a. 4m b. -40m c. -0.25m d. -25m

   Answer c

   5. A concave mirror gives virtual, refract and enlarged image of the object but image of smaller size than the size

of the object is

   a. At infinity b. Between F and C c. Between P and F d. At E

   Answer c

   6. In optics an object which has higher refractive index is called

   a. Optically rarer b. optically denser c. Optical density d. Refractive index

   Answer b

   7. The optical phenomena, twinkling of stars, is due to

   a. Atmospheric reflection b. Total reflection c. Atmospheric refraction d. Total refraction

   Answer c

   8. Convex lens focus a real, point sized image at focus, the object is placed

   a. At focus b. Between F and 2F c. At infinity d. At 2F

   Answer c

   9. The unit of power of lens is

   a. Metre b. Centimetre c. Dioptre d. M-1

   Answer c

   10. The radius of curvature of a mirror is 20cm the focal length is

   a. 20cm b. 10cm c. 40cm d. 5cm

   Answer b

   11. Identify the factor on which the angle of deviation of the prism does not depend.

   a) The angle of incidence b) The material of the prism

   c) The angle of reflection d) The wavelength of light used

   Answer: c

   12. What is the relative refractive index of water with respect to glass?

a) Unity b) More than unity c) Less than unity d) Zero

Answer: c

13. The refraction in a water tank makes apparent depth the same throughout.

a) True b) False

Answer: c

14. What will be the colour of the sky in the absence of the atmosphere?

a) White b) Dark c) Blue d) Pink

Answer: b

15. A lens immersed in a transparent liquid is not visible. Under what condition can this happen?

a) Less refractive index b) Higher refractive index

c) Same refractive index d) Total internal reflection is zero

Answer: c

16. What is the cause of the blue colour of the ocean?

a) Reflection b) Scattering of light by water molecules c) Total internal reflection d) Refraction

Answer: b

17. What causes haloes (rings) around the sun or the moon?

a) Total internal reflection b) Refraction of light c) Reflection of light d) Dispersion

Answer: c

18. Why is the sequence of colours in the secondary rainbow reverse of that in the primary rainbow?

a) Refraction of light b) Two internal reflection c) Reflection of light d) Dispersion

Answer: b

19. Identify the principle behind the sparkling of diamonds.

a) Total internal reflection b) Refraction c) Reflection d) Optical activity

Answer: a

20. The secondary rainbow is brighter than the primary rainbow.

a) True b) False

Answer: b

3.20 Important Questions

1. What is refraction? Define refractive index.
2. Define refractive index in terms of wavelength of light.
3. What is meant by relative refractive index of medium?
4. State the factors on which the refractive index of a medium depends.
5. State Snell's law of refraction of light.
6. When does Snell's law of refraction fail?
7. For which material the value of refractive index is: (i) minimum and (ii) maximum?
8. What is lateral shift in refraction?
9. On what factors does the lateral shift depend?
10. For what angle of incidence, the lateral shift produced by a parallel sided glass slab is zero?
11. Light of wavelength 6000 Å in air enters a medium of refractive index 1.5. What will be its frequency in the medium?
12. When light undergoes refraction, what happens to its frequency?
13. When light undergoes refraction at the surface of separation of two media, what happens to its wavelength?
14. How does the frequency of a beam of ultraviolet light change when it goes from air into glass?
15. Define the term critical angle for a pair of media.
16. Can total internal reflection occur when light travels from a rarer to a denser medium?

17. Velocity of light in glass 2 x 10^8 m/s and in air is 3×10^8 m/s. If the ray of light passes from glass to air, calculate the value of critical angle.
18. A substance has a critical angle of 45° for yellow light. What is its refractive index?
19. 45. Which one has a greater critical angle-diamond or water?
20. A good plane mirror reflects about 95% of light. What is the percentage of light reflected when total internal reflection occurs?
21. Write the relation between the refractive index k and critical angle for a given pair of optical media.
22. When light is incident on a rarer medium from a denser medium, write the relation between the critical angle and refractive indices of two media.
23. State the conditions under which total internal reflection occurs.
24. What is an optical fibre? Which of the two main parts of an optical fibre has a higher value of refractive index? Name the physical principle on which the working of optical fibres is based.
25. What is the main use of optical fibres?
26. What is a lens? Define optical centre of a lens.
27. What is the deviation produced by a thin lens of a ray passing through its optical centre?
28. What type of a lens is a tumbler filled with water?
29. Can a lens be used in a medium of which it is made of?
30. A lens always forms virtual and erect image of the object irrespective of the position of the object. What type of lens is this?
31. Where an object should be placed from a convex lens to form an image of the same size? Can it happen in case of concave lens?
32. Define power of a lens. Give its Sl units.
33. Define refractive index of a material: Give its physical significance.
34. Distinguish between absolute refractive index and relative refractive index of a material. Write a relation between these refractive indices.
35. Explain the cause of refraction of light.
36. A ray of light bends towards normal as it passes from air to glass. Give reason.
37. Discuss the refraction through a glass-slab and show that the emergent ray is parallel to the incident ray but laterally displaced.
38. Explain why does a water tank appear shallower?
39. An object placed at the bottom of a beaker containing water appears to be raised. Why?
40. Light travels from air in to glass slab of thickness 50 cm and refractive index 1.5.

    i) What is the speed of light in glass?
    ii) What is the time taken by the light to travel through the glass slab?
    iii) What is the optical path of the glass slab?

1. Light travelling through transparent oil enters in to glass of refractive index 1.5. If the refractive index of glass with respect to the oil is 1.25, what is the refractive index of the oil?
2. A coin is at the bottom of a trough containing three immiscible liquids of refractive indices 1.3, 1.4 and 1.5 poured one above the other of heights 30 cm, 16 cm, and 20 cm respectively. What is the apparent depth at which the coin appears to be when seen from air medium outside? In which medium the coin will be seen?

Chapter 4: Electrostatics

Chapter 4: Electrostatics

4.1 Introduction:

Electrostatics. Electrostatics is the study of electric charges at rest. Here we study the forces, fields and potentials associated with static charges. Coulomb's law describes electrostatic processes, which result from the forces that electric charges apply to one another. Even if forces generated by electrostatics appear to be rather little.

In many ways electrostatics has been a neglected science because static electricity has never been considered as useful as "current electricity". This is changing in the industrial world partly because static electricity represents a costly problem in many areas of manufacturing, but also because static electricity can be used productively in new industrial methods and processes. There are literally hundreds of well-known examples of electrostatic phenomena from the classic balloon stuck to a wall or raising your hair, to the attraction of polystyrene balls or plastic wrapping when it is being torn from a package.

Applications of electrostatics: The attraction and repulsion between charged bodies have many industrial applications. Some of these are as follows:

1. In electrostatic loudspeaker.
2. In electrostatic spraying of paints and powder coating.
3. In fly ash collection in chimneys.
4. In a Xerox copying machine.
5. In the design of a cathode-ray tube used in television and radar.
6. Smoke Precipitators and Electrostatic Air Cleaning
7. The Van de Graff Generator. e.t.c

Two kinds of electric charges:
About 100 years ago, Charles Du Fay of France showed that electric charges on various objects are of normally two kinds. The following simple experiments prove this fact.
Experiment 1
(i) Rub a glass rod with silk and suspend it from a rigid support by means of a silk thread. Bring another similarly charged rod near it. The two rods repel each other Fig. 4.1(a).

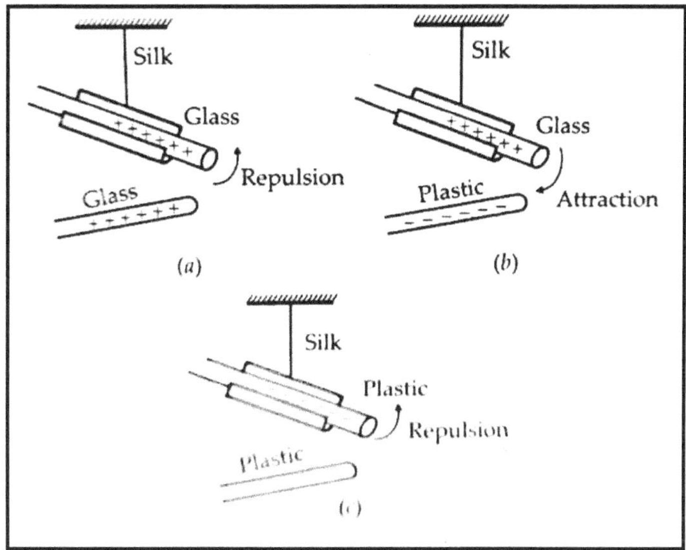

Fig, 4.1 like charges repel and unlike charges attract each other.

(ii) Bring a plastic rod rubbed with wool near the charged glass rod. The two rods attract each other Fig. 4.1(b).

(iii) Now rub a plastic rod with wool and suspend it from a rigid support. Bring another similarly charged plastic rod near it. There will be a repulsion between the two rods Fig. 4.1(c).

Experiment 2

If a glass rod, rubbed with silk, is made to touch two small pith balls (or polystyrene balls) which are suspended by silk threads, then the two balls repel each other, as shown in Fig. 4.2(a). Similarly, two pith balls touched with a plastic rod rubbed with fur are found to repel each other [Fig. 4.2(b)]. But it is seen that a pith ball touched with glass rod attracts another pith ball touched with a plastic rod [Fig. 4.2(c)].

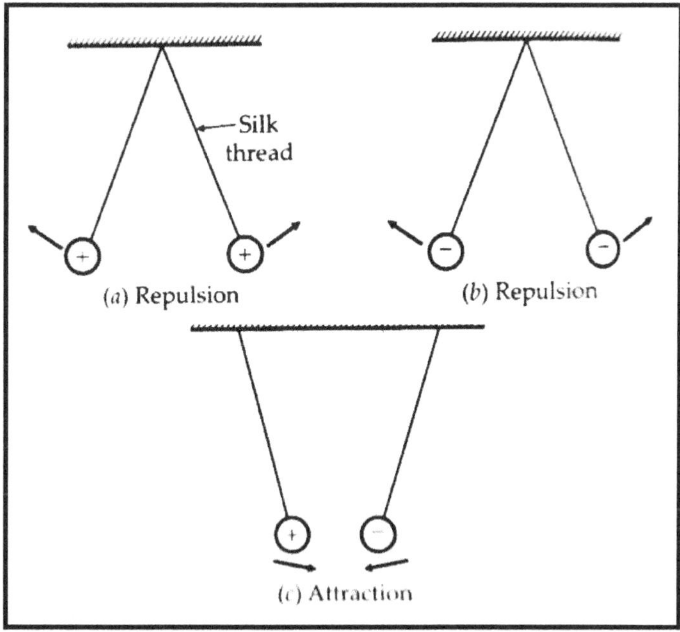

Fig. 4.2 like charges repel and unlike charges attract.

From the above experiments, we note that the charge produced on a glass rod is different from the charge produced on a plastic rod. Also the charge produced on a pith ball touched with a glass rod is different from the charge produced on pith ball touched with a plastic rod. We can conclude that:

1. There are only two kinds of electric charges –positive and negative.

2. Like charges repel and unlike charges attract each other.

The statement 2 is known as the fundamental law of electrostatics. The above experiments also demonstrate that the charges are transferred from the rods to the pith balls on contact, we say that the pith balls have been electrified or charged by contact, this property which distinguishes the two kinds of charges is called the polarity of charge.

4.2 Electric charge:

Electric charge is an intrinsic property of the elementary particles like electrons, protons, etc. of which all the objects are made up of. It is because of these electric charges that various objects exert strong electric forces of attraction or repulsion on each other. Electric charge is an intrinsic property of elementary particles of matter which gives rise to electric force between various objects.

Electric charge is a fundamental property of matter that determines how it interacts with electromagnetic fields. When charges are stationary, they produce an electric field around them, and when in motion, they produce a magnetic field as well. Electric charge comes in two types: positive and negative. Like charges repel whereas unlike charges attract.

Electric charge is a scalar quantity. Its SI unit is coulomb (C). A proton has a positive charge $(+ e)$ and an electron has a negative charge $(-e)$, where $e = 1.6 \times 10^{-19}$ coulomb.

4.3 Basic properties of electric charge

It is observed from experiments that electric charge has following three basic properties:

1. Additivity, 2. Quantization, 3. Conservation.

1. Additivity of electric charge:

Additive nature of electric charges, Like mass, electric charge is a scalar quantity. Just as the mass of an extended body is the sum of the masses of its individual particles, the total charge of an extended body is the algebraic sum (i.e., the sum taking into account the positive and negative signs) of all the charges located at different points inside it. Thus, the electric charge is additive in nature.

Additivity of electric charge means that the total charge of a system is the algebraic sum of all the individual charges located at different points inside the system.

If a system contains charges $q_1, q_2, \ldots \ldots q_n$, then its total charge is

$q = q_1 + q_2 + \ldots \ldots + q_n$ **4.1**

The total charge of a system containing four charges $2\ \mu C$, $-3\ \mu C$, $4\ \mu C$ and $-5\ \mu C$ is

$q = 2\ \mu C - 3\ \mu C + 4\ \mu C - 5\ \mu C = -2\ \mu C$

2. Quantization of a physical quantity:

The quantization of a physical quantity means that it cannot vary continuously to have any arbitrary value but it can change discontinuously to take any one of only a discrete set of values, For example, a building can have different floors (ground, first, second, etc.) from the ground floor upwards but it cannot have a floor of the value in-between. Thus the energy of an electron in atom or the electric charge of a system is quantized, the minimum amount by which a physical quantity can change is called its quantum.

Quantization of electric charge. It is found experimentally that the electric charge of any body, large or small, is always an integral multiple of a certain minimum amount of charge. This basic charge is the charge on an electron, which is denoted by e and has magnitude 1.6×10^{-19} coulomb. Thus the charge on an electron is $-e$ on a proton is $+e$ and that on a particle is $+ 2e$.

The experimental fact that electric charges occur in discrete amounts instead of continuous amounts is called quantization of electric charge. The quantization of electric charge means that the total charge (q) of a body is always an integral multiple of a basic quantum of charge (e), i.e,

q=ne, where n=0, ± 1, ±2, ±3,........ 4.2

Cause of quantization:

The basic cause of quantization of electric charge is that during rubbing only an integral number of electrons can be transferred from one body to another. Quantization of electric charge is an experimentally verified law:

1. The experimental laws of electrolysis discovered by Faraday first suggested the quantization of electric charge.

2. Millikan's oil drop experiment in 1912 on the measurement of electric charge further established the quantization of electric charge.

When can we ignore the quantization of electric charge: While dealing with macroscopic charges (q= ne), can ignore the quantization of electric charge. This is because the basic charge e is very small and n is very large in most practical situations, so g behaves as if it were continuous i.e., as if a large amount of charge were flowing. For example, when we switch on a 60 W bulb, nearly 2 x 10 electrons pass through its filament per second. Here the graininess or structure of charge does not show up i.e., the bulb does not flicker with the entry of each electron. Quantization of charge becomes important at the microscopic level, where the charges involved are of the order of a few tens or hundreds of e.

3. Conservation of charge

Law of conservation of charge: If some amount of matter is isolated in a certain region of space and no matter either enters or leaves this region by moving across its boundary, then whatever other changes may occur in the matter inside, its total charge will not change with time. This is the law of conservation of charge which states:

1. The total charge of an isolated system remains constant.

2. The electric charges can neither be created nor destroyed, they can only be transferred from one body to another.

The law of conservation of charge is obeyed both in large scale and microscopic processes. In fact, charge conservation is a global phenomenon i.e., total charge of the entire universe remains constant.

Examples:

1. When a glass rod is rubbed with a silk cloth. It develops a positive charge. But at the same time, the silk cloth develops an equal negative charge. Thus the net charge of the glass rod and the silk cloth is zero, as it was before rubbing.

2. The rock salt ionises in aqueous solution as follows:

$NaCl=Na^+ + Cl^-$

As the total charge is zero before and after the ionisation, so charge is conserved.

3. Charge is conserved during the fission of a $^{235}U_{92}$ nucleus by a neutron.

$$_0^1 n + _{92}^{235} U \rightarrow _{56}^{141} Ba + _{36}^{92} Kr + 3 _0^1 n + Energy$$

Total charge before fission (0 + 92)=Total charge after fission (56 + 36 +3x 0)

4. Electric charge is conserved during the phenomenon of pair production in which a y-ray photon materialises into an electron-positron pair.

$$\gamma - ray (zero\ charge) \rightarrow electron(-e) + positron(+e)$$

5. In annihilation of matter, an electron and a positron on coming in contact destroy each other, producing two y-ray photons, each of energy 0.51 MeV.

$$electron(-e) + positron(+e) \rightarrow 2Y - ray(zero\ charge)$$

Where & is called permittivity of free space. So we can express Coulomb's law in SI units as

Units of charge

(i) The SI unit of charge is coulomb. In the above equation, if q1 =q2 =1C and r=1 m, then

$$F = \frac{1}{4\pi\varepsilon_0} = 9\times10^9\,N$$

4.2

So one coulomb is that amount of charge that repels an equal and similar charge with a force of 9 x 10^9 N when placed in vacuum at a distance of one metre from it.

(ii) In electrostatic cgs system, the unit of charge is known as electrostatic unit of charge (e.s.u. of charge) or stat coulomb (stat C).

One e.s.u. of charge or one stat coulomb is that charge which repels an identical charge in vacuum at a distance of one centimetre from it with a force of 1 dyne.

1 coulomb =3x 10^9 stat-coulomb 4.3

=3x 10^9 e.s.u. of charge

(iii) In electromagnetic cgs system, the unit of charge is abcoulomb or electromagnetic unit of charge (e.m.u. of charge).

1 coulomb = 1/10 abcoulomb = 1/10 e.m.u. of charge.

Types of Charged Particles

There are primarily two types of charged particles which are discussed below:

i) Positively Charged Particles

Protons are the positively charged particles that are found in the nucleus of an atom. Protons have a mass of about 1 u. A particle gain positive charge when it lose electrons.

ii) Negatively Charged Particles

Electrons are negatively charged subatomic particles that surround the nucleus of an atom. Electrons have a much smaller mass of about 0.0005u. Electrons are located outside the nucleus in the outermost regions of the atom, called electron shells. A particle gain negative charge when its gains electron from other particle

After from positive and negatively charged particles, there are neutral particles:

iii) Neutral Particles

Neutrons are Neutral subatomic particles that are also found in the nucleus of an atom. Neutrons have a mass of about 1 u.

Charge Distributions:

In electrostatics we deal with point charges and different types of charge distributions -volume charge distribution, line charge distribution, and surface charge distribution.

Volume Charge Distribution: Volume Charge Distribution is visualised as a region of space filled with vary large number of discrete particles (electrons or atoms) separated by finite atomic distances. The assumption of this being a continuous charge does not involve much errors. The volume charge distribution is described in terms of volume charge density (ρ_v), C/m³. An example of such a distribution is the space between the control grid and the cathode

in the electron-gun assembly of a cathode-ray tube operating with space charge.
The volume charge density is defined as

$$\rho_v = \lim_{\Delta v \to 0} \frac{\Delta q}{\Delta v} \ \text{C/m}^3$$

4.4

Where Δq is small amount of charge in a small volume Δv.
The total charge within a defined volume is obtained by taking the volume integral throughout that volume.

$$q = \int_v dq = \int_v \rho_v\, dv$$

4.5

Where q is the total charge and represents the volume integral. A volume integral involves three integrations, can also be written as.

Line Charge Distribution: Line Charge Distribution is visualised as filament like distribution of a volume charge density, such as a very thin sharp beam in a cathode-raytube. It can also be considered as charge distribution on a very thin conductor ($r \to 0$). The line charge distribution is described in terms of line charge density $(.\lambda_l)$, C/m.

The line charge density λ_l is defined as

$$\lambda_l = \lim_{\Delta l \to 0} \frac{\Delta q}{\Delta l} \ \text{C/m}$$

4.6

Where Δq is small amount of charge in elemental length Δl
The total charge q is obtained by line integral of line charge density, as below

$$q = \int_l dq = \int_l \lambda_l\, dl$$

4.7

Surface (Sheet) Charge Distribution: Surface (Sheet) Charge Distribution is visualised as charge distributed on a conducting sheet like the charge on the plates of a capacitor. The surface charge distribution is described in terms of surface charge density (σ_s), C/m^2.

The surface charge density σ_s is defined as

• 77 •

$$\sigma_z = \lim_{\Delta s \to 0} \frac{\Delta q}{\Delta s} \ \text{C/m}^2$$

4.8

Where Δq is small amount of charge on small surface Δs.

The total charge q on a defined surface is obtained by taking the surface integral over the complete surface.

$$q = \int_s dq = \int_s \sigma_z d\vec{l}$$

4.9

4.4 Coulomb's Law of force:

For those not familiar with Charles-Augustin de Coulomb or why the study of electrostatics is in his debt, in 1785 he published the first of three reports in which he defined the law by which scientists could finally understand the forces at work in electrostatic interaction.

Coulomb's law: Coulomb's law states that "the magnitude of the electrostatic force of interaction between two point charges is directly proportional to the scalar multiplication of the magnitudes of charges and inversely proportional to the square of the distance between them. The force is along the straight line joining them. If the two charges have the same sign, the electrostatic force between them is repulsive; if they have different signs, the force between them is attractive."

Roughly translated this means that the closer two charges are, the stronger the force between them.

The Coulomb (unit symbol: C) was then adopted as the international system of units (SI), unit of electric charge.

Fig 4.3 Force between two charge

If q1 and q2 are two point charges, separated by a distance r, then the force between them

$$F \prec \frac{q_1 q_2}{r^2}$$

$$F = K \frac{q_1 q_2}{r^2}$$

4.10

With charges given in coulomb and distance in meter the force F is in newton (N). K is constant of proportionality. In the International System, the constant of proportionality is given by

$$K = \frac{1}{4\pi\varepsilon}$$

4.11

Where ε is the permittivity of the medium where charges are situated. The permittivity of the medium is also called dielectric constant with unit as farad per meter (F/m). The permittivity of free space or vacuum is

$$\varepsilon_0 = 8.854 \times 10^{-12} F/m$$

4.12

Permittivity: An introduction. When two charges are placed in any medium other than air, the force between them is greatly affected. Permittivity is a property of the medium which determines the electric force between two charges situated in that medium. For example, 2 the force between two charges located some distance apart in water is about $1/80^{th}$ of the force between them when they are separated by same distance in air. This is because the absolute permittivity of water is about 80 times greater than the absolute permittivity of air or free space.

In general, the permittivity of a medium is given with respect to the permittivity of free space (vacuum), as

$$\varepsilon = \varepsilon_r \varepsilon_0$$

$$4.13$$

Where E, is the relative permittivity with values equal to or greater than 1 and ε, is the permittivity of vacuum. For vacuum ε_0 =1, for air ε_r=1. For air we may write

$$K = \frac{1}{4\pi\varepsilon} = \frac{1}{4\pi\varepsilon_0\varepsilon_r} = 9\times10^9\,F/m$$

$$4.14$$

From Coulomb's experiments, the following other conclusions were reached beside the one's given above : (i) like charges repel whereas unlike charges attract, (ii) the direction of force is along the line joining the charges, and (iii) the force depends upon the medium in which the charges are placed. Substituting the value of K in (4.10) and writing the force as vector

$$\overline{F} = \frac{q_1q_2}{4\pi\varepsilon r^2}\,\hat{n}$$

$$4.15$$

It is the Coulomb force that binds the electrons of an atom to its nucleus, the atoms into molecules and the atoms of molecules into large aggregation of liquid or solid form. The Coulomb's law is linear. The force at a point charge due to two or more charges can be added vectorially.

Limitations of Coulomb's law:

Coulomb's law is not applicable in all situations. It is valid only under the following conditions:

1. The electric charges must be at rest.
2. The electric charges must be point charges i.e. the extension of charges must be much smaller than the separation between the charges.
3. The separation between the charges must be greater than the nuclear size (10m), because for distances < 10m, the strong nuclear force dominates over the electrostatic force.

Vector Form of Coulomb's law of Force:

q_1 and q_2 are two point charges, separated by a distance r_{21}. The distance of charge q_1 from origin o is r_1 and distance of charge q_2 from origin is r_2. Then the force between them

$$\overline{F} = \frac{q_1 q_2}{4\pi\varepsilon r^2}\,\hat{r}$$

$$\overline{F} = \frac{q_1 q_2}{4\pi\varepsilon r^3}\,\overline{r}$$

4.16

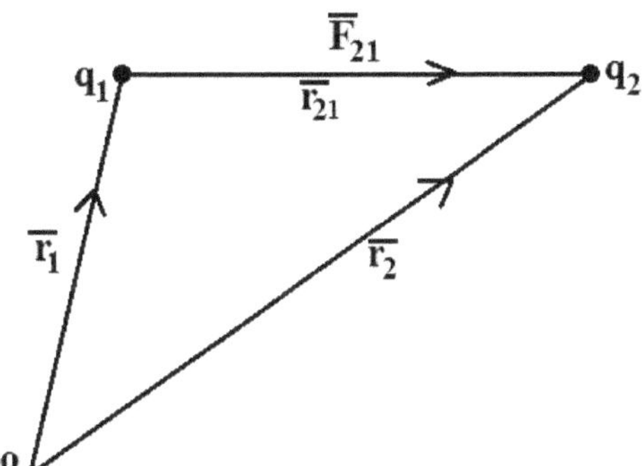

Fig 4.4 q_1 and q_2 are two point charges, separated by a distance r_{21}

From the fig 4.4 as per vector addition we can write

$$\overline{r_1} + \overline{r_{21}} = \overline{r_2}$$

$$\overline{r_{21}} = \overline{r_2} - \overline{r_1}$$

$$and$$

$$\hat{r}_{21} = \frac{\overline{r_{21}}}{\left|\overline{r_{21}}\right|} = \frac{\overline{r_2} - \overline{r_1}}{\left|\overline{r_2} - \overline{r_1}\right|}$$

4.17

Substituting the value from equation 4.17 to 4.16 we get,

$$\overline{F} = \frac{q_1 q_2}{4\pi\varepsilon \left|\overline{r_2} - \overline{r_1}\right|^3}\left(\overline{r_2} - \overline{r_1}\right)$$

4.18

Equation 4.18 represent the vector form of Coulomb's law of force.

4.5 Electric field intensity (E)

Consider a positive charge q1 placed rigidly at the origin of a spherical coordinate system. If another positive point charge q2 call it a test charge, is brought into the vicinity of q1 it will be acted upon by a force

$$\overline{F_{21}} = \frac{q_1 q_2}{4\pi\varepsilon_0 r_{21}^{\,2}} \, \hat{r}_{21}$$

4.19

r is the distance between q1 and q2 and r21 is outward unit vector at q2 giving the direction of force.

The force is radially outward and increases as q2 approaches q1. It may be said that q1 has a field around it which exerts force on another charge. This field is called an Electric Field due to q1 (by which other charges experience force).

Rewriting (4.19) as force per unit charge gives

$$\frac{\overline{F_{21}}}{q_2} = \frac{q_1}{4\pi\varepsilon_0 r_{21}^{\,2}} \, \hat{r}_{21}$$

4.20

This quantity, "Force per unit charge is called Electric Field Intensity, E". It is a vector force on a unit positive test charge.

Electric field: An electric field is said to exist at a point if a force of electrical origin is exerted on a stationary charged body placed at that point. Quantitatively, the electric field or the electric intensity or the electric field strength E at a point is defined as the force experienced by a unit positive test charge placed at that point, without disturbing the position of source charge.

$$E = \frac{\overline{F_{21}}}{q_2} = \frac{q_1}{4\pi\varepsilon_0 r_{21}^{\,2}} \, \hat{r}_{21}$$

Or in general

$$\frac{\overline{F_{21}}}{q_2} = \frac{q_1}{4\pi\varepsilon_0 r_{21}^2}\, \hat{r}_{21}$$

$$\overline{E} = \frac{\overline{F}}{q} = \frac{q}{4\pi\varepsilon_0 r^2}\, \hat{r}$$

4.21

The SI unit of electric field intensity is newton per coulomb (N/C). Another unit of electric field intensity is volt per meter (V/m).

The nature of the field around a point charge is shown in Fig. 4.5 in the vector form, the vector being proportional to force at the point.

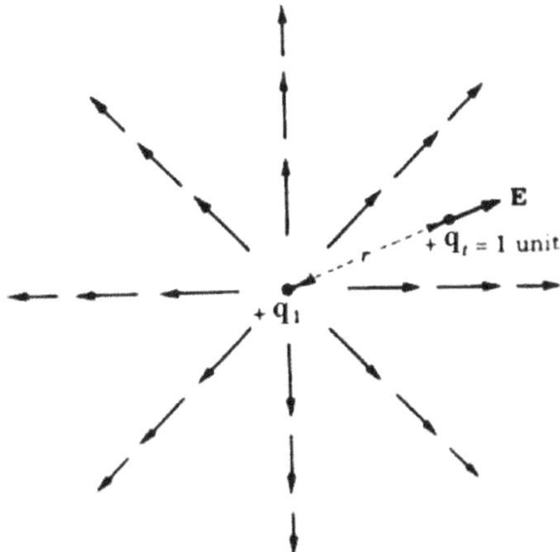

Fig. 4.5 the electric field associated with a point charge q1 derived from a vector force on a test charge.

The test charge need not be one unit, but can be much smaller, may be regarded as of infinitesimal size, and the field at a point becomes the ratio of force ΔF (on it) to the positive test charge Δq with the limit Δq approaches zero.

$$\overline{E} = \lim_{\Delta q \to 0} \frac{\Delta \overline{F}}{\Delta q}$$

4.22

The electric field at a point is defined as the electrostatic force per unit test charge acting on a vanishingly small positive test charge placed at that point. The electric field É is a vector quantity whose direction is same as that of the force F exerted on a positive test charge.

Physical significance of electric field: The force experienced by the test charge go is different at different points. So E also varies from point to point. In general, E is not a single vector but a set of infinite vectors. Each point r is associated with a unique vector E (r). So electric field is an example of vector field. By knowing electric field at any point, we can determine the force on a charge placed at that point.

The Coulomb force on a charge 4o due to a source charge q_0 may be treated as two stage process:

(1) The source charge q produces a definite field É(r) at every point r.

(ii) The value of E(r) at any point r determines the force on charge 4o at that point. This force is

F=q_0E(r)

Electrostatic force = Charge x Electric field.

Thus an electric field plays an intermediary role in the forces between two charges:

$$Charge \rightleftharpoons Electric\ Field \rightleftharpoons Charge$$

It is in this sense that the concept of electric field is useful. Electric field is a characteristic of the system of c charges and is independent of the test charge that we place at a point to determine the field.

4.6 Electric lines of force:

Michael Faraday (1791-1867) introduced the concept of lines of force to visualize the nature of electric (and magnetic) fields. A small positive charge placed in an electric field experiences a force in a definite direction and if it is free to move, it will start moving in that direction. The path along which this charge would move will be a line of force.

Definition: An electric line of force may be defined as the curve along which a small positive charge would tend to move when free to do so in an electric field and the tangent to which at any point gives the direction of the electric field at that point.

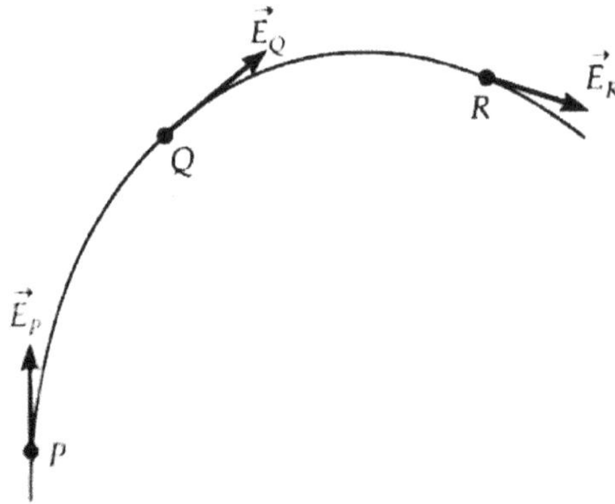

Fig 4.6 an electric line of force.

In Fig. 4.6 the curve POR is an electric line of force. The tangent drawn to this curve at the point P gives the direction of the field E, at the point P. Similarly, the tangent at the point Q gives the direction of the field E at the point Q and so on.

The lines of force do not really exist, they are imaginary curves. Yet the concept of lines of force is very useful. Michael Faraday gave simple explanations for many of his discoveries (in electricity and magnetism) in terms of such lines of force.

Properties of Electric Lines of Force

1. The lines of force are continuous smooth curves without any breaks,

2. The lines of force start at positive charges and end at negative charges - they cannot form closed loops, If there is a single charge, then the lines of force will start or end at infinity.

3. The tangent to a line of force at any point gives the direction of the electric field at that point.

4. No two lines of force can cross each other.

5. The lines of force are always normal to the surface of a conductor on which the charges are in equilibrium.

6. The lines of force have a tendency to contract lengthwise. This explains attraction between two unlike charges.

7. The lines of force have a tendency to expand laterally so as to exert a lateral pressure on neighbouring lines of force. This explains repulsion between two similar charges.

8. The relative closeness of the lines of force gives a measure of the strength of the electric field in any region. The lines of force are

(i) close together in a strong field.

(ii) far apart in a weak field.

(ii) parallel and equally spaced in a uniform field.

9. The lines of force do not pass through a conductor because the electric field inside a charged conductor is zero.

Electric field lines for different charged conductors:

(i) Field lines of a positive point charge. Fig. 4.7 shows the lines of force of an isolated positive point charge, they are directed radially outwards because a small positive charge would be accelerated in the outward direction. They extend to infinity. The field is spherically symmetric i.e, it looks same in all directions, as seen from the point charge.

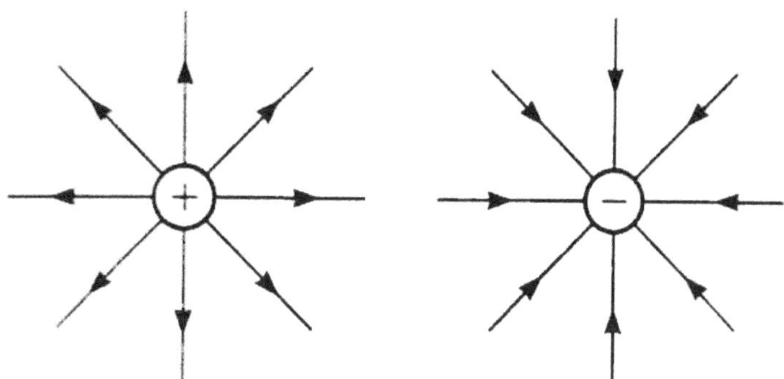

Fig. 4.7 Field lines of a positive and negative point charge.

(ii) Field lines of a negative point charge. Like that of a positive point charge, the electric field of a negative point charge is also spherically symmetric but the lines of force point radially inwards as shown in Fig. 4.7. They start from infinity.

(iii) Field lines of two equal and opposite point charges. Fig. 4.8 shows the electric lines of force of an electric dipole i.e, a system of two equal and opposite point charges (+ q) separated by a small distance. They start from the positive charge and end on the negative charge. The lines of force seem to contract lengthwise as if the two charges are being pulled together. This explains attraction between two unlike charges. The field is cylindrically symmetric about the dipole axis i.e., the field pattern is same in all planes passing through the dipole axis. Clearly, the electric field at all points on the equatorial line is parallel to the axis of the dipole.

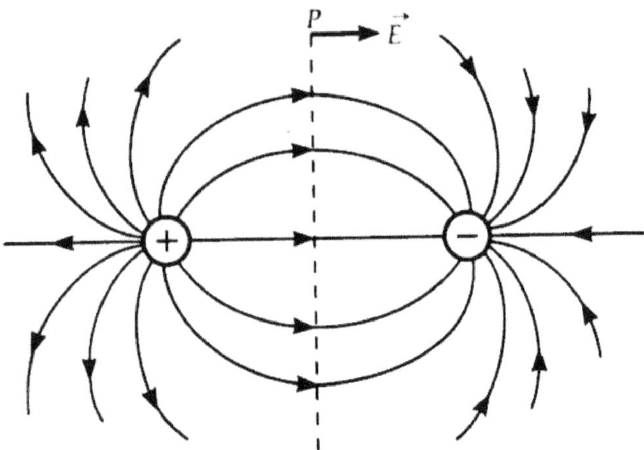

Fig, 4.8 Field lines of an electric dipole.

(iv) Field lines of two equal and positive point charges. Fig 4.9 shows the lines of force of two equal and positive point charges. They seem to exert a lateral pressure as if the two charges are being pushed away from each other, this explains repulsion between two like charges, The field E is zero at the middle point N of the join of two charges. This point is called neutral point from which no line of force passes, this field also has cylindrical symmetry.

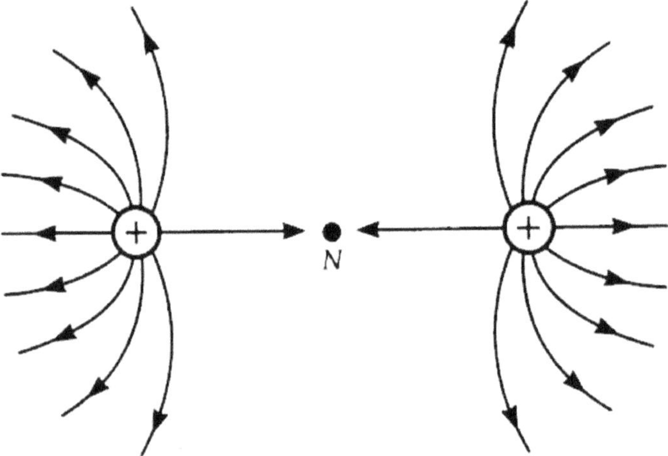

Fig. 4.9 Field lines of two equal positive charges.

(v) Field lines of a positively charged plane conductor. Fig. 4.10 shows the pattern of lines of force of positively charged plane conductor. A small positive charge would tend to move normally away from the plane conductor. Thus the lines of force are parallel and normal to the surface of the conductor. They are equispaced, indicating that electric field É is uniform at all points near the plane conductor.

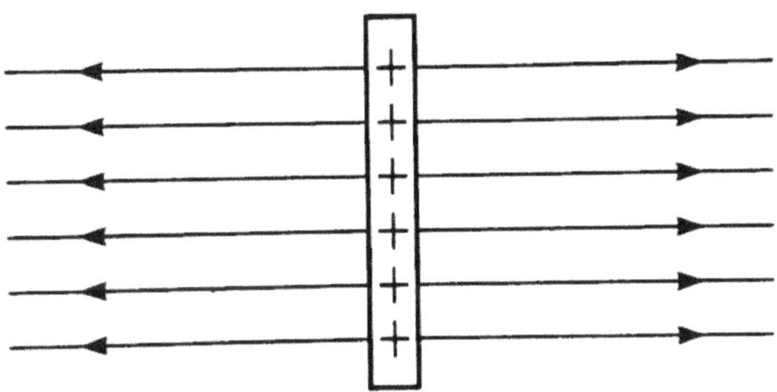

Fig. 4.10 Field pattern of a positively charged plane conductor.

Relation between electric field strength and density of lines of force. Electric field strength is proportional to the density of lines of force i.e., electric field strength at a point is proportional to the number of lines of force cutting a unit area element placed normal to the field at that point. As illustrated in Fig. 4.11, the electric field at P is stronger than at Q.

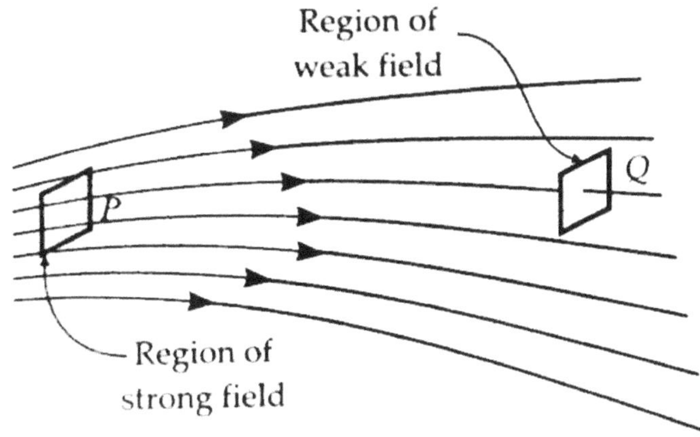

Fig. 4.11 Density of lines of force is proportional to the electric field strength.

4.7 Electric flux

The term flux implies some kind of flow. Flux is the property of any vector field. The electric flux is a property of electric field. The electric flux through a given area held inside an electric field is the measure of the total number of electric lines of force passing normally through that area.

As shown in Fig. 4.12, if an electric field E passes normally through an area element AS, then the electric flux through this area is

$$\Delta\phi_E = E\,\Delta S$$

4.23

4.23

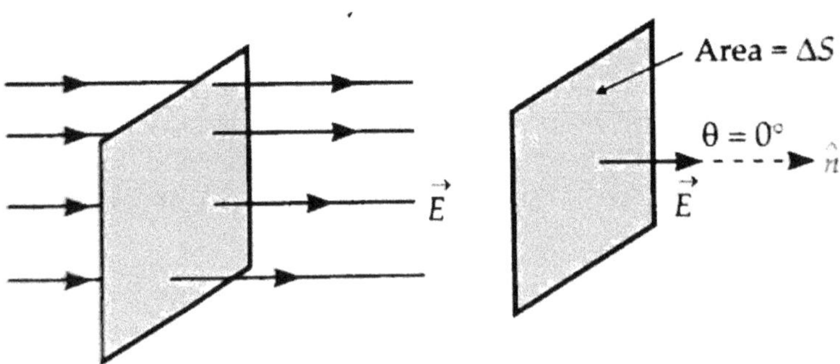

Fig 4.12 Electric flux through normal area.

As shown in Fig 4.12, if the normal drawn to the area element ΔS makes an angle Θ with the uniform field E, then the component of E normal to ΔS will be Ecos Θ, so that the electric flux is

$$\Delta\phi_E = Normal\ component\ of\ E \times Surface\ area$$
$$\Delta\phi_E = E\cos\theta \times \Delta S$$
$$\Delta\phi_E = E\Delta S\cos\theta$$
$$\Delta\phi_E = \overline{E}\cdot\overline{\Delta S}$$

4.24

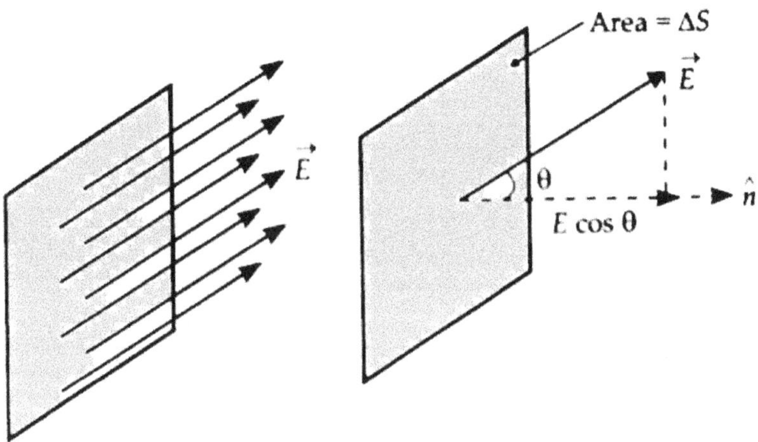

Fig. 4.13 Flux through an inclined area.

In case the field E is non-uniform, we consider a closed surface S lying inside the field, as shown in
Fig. 4.14. Thus the electric flux through any surface S, open or closed, is equal to the surface integral of the electric field Ë taken over the surface S.

$$\Delta \phi_E = \oint \overline{E} \bullet \Delta \overline{S}$$

4.25

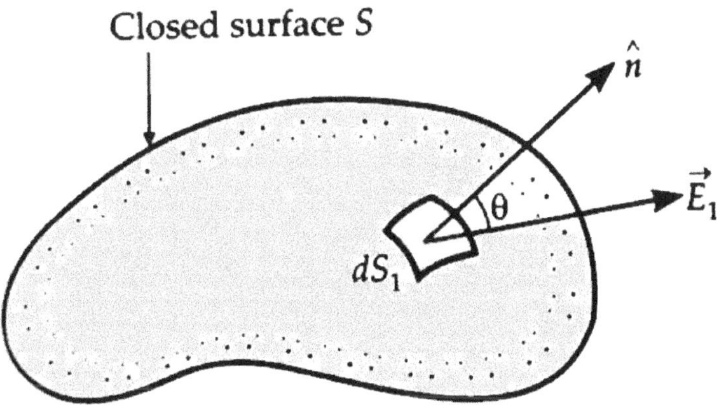

Fig. 4.14 Electric Flux through a closed surface

Electric flux is a scalar quantity. SI unit of electric flux is $NC^{-1}.m^2$.

4.8 Gauss's Theorem

This theorem gives a relationship between the total lux passing through any closed surface and the net charge enclosed within the surface.

Gauss theorem states that the total flux through a closed surface is $1/\varepsilon_0$, times the net charge enclosed by the closed surface.

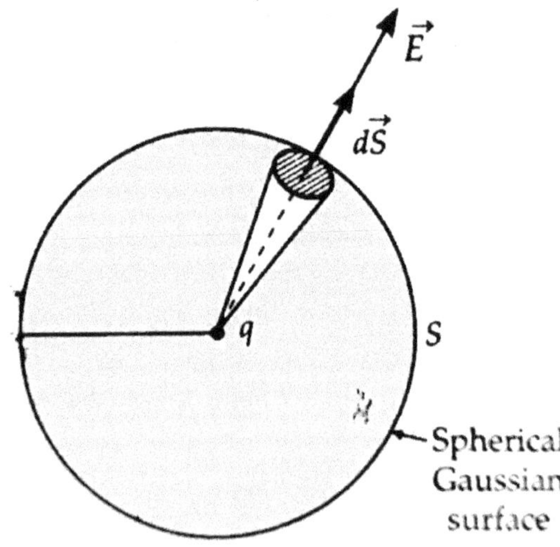

Fig 4.15: Flux through a sphere enclosing a point charge

Mathematically, it can be expressed as

$$\phi_E = \oiint \overline{E}\cdot d\overline{S} = \frac{q}{\varepsilon_0}$$

4.26

4.9 Application of Gauss law to find electric field due to a charged sphere

Electric field due to uniformly charged sphere: This is the case of solid non-conducting spheres. We will have three cases associated with it. They are: electric fields inside the sphere, on the surface, outside the sphere. Apply the gauss theorem to find the electric field at the three different places. Consider a charged solid sphere of radius R and charge q which is uniformly distributed over the sphere. We will use Gauss Theorem to calculate electric fields. If ϕ be the electric flux and Q be the charge then; $\varepsilon_0\phi = Q_{enclosed}$

Also electric flux=electric field X area of the enclosed surface : $\phi = EA$

i) Case I- Inside the sphere (r<R)

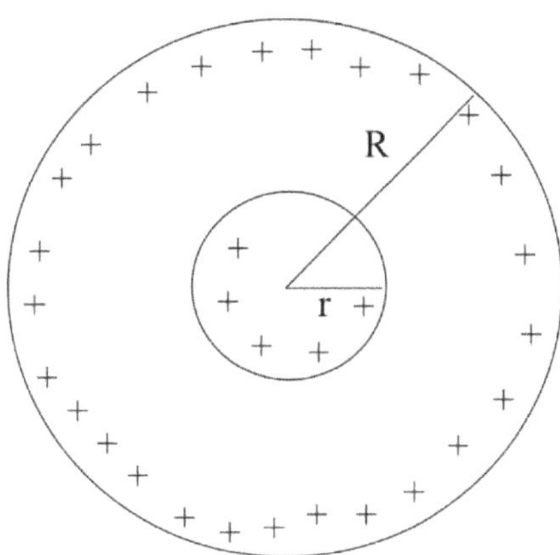

Fig 4.16 Field for a point inside the sphere

The charge distribution is uniform. Volume density will be the same. Let the charge enclosed by a circle of radius r be q'. Since volume density is same then-

$$\frac{q'}{\frac{4}{3}\pi r^3} = \frac{q}{\frac{4}{3}\pi R^3}$$

$$q' = q\,\frac{r^3}{R^3}$$

4.27

Applying Gauss Theorem here-

$$\phi = E4\pi r^2$$

$$\frac{Q_{enclosed}}{\varepsilon_0} = E4\pi r^2$$

$$\phi = E4\pi r^2$$

$$\frac{Q_{enclosed}}{\varepsilon_0} = E4\pi r^2$$

hence

$$\frac{q'}{\varepsilon_0} = E4\pi r^2$$

4.28

$$\frac{q'}{\varepsilon_0} \times \frac{r^3}{R^3} = E4\pi r^2$$

$$E = \frac{1}{4\pi\varepsilon_0} \times \frac{qr}{R^3}$$

4.29

This is the electric field inside the charged sphere.

Case II: On the surface (r=R)

In the above case we have calculated the electric field inside the sphere. In that formula we will put (r=R), so evaluate the electric field on the surface of the sphere.

$$E = \frac{1}{4\pi\varepsilon_0} \times \frac{q}{R^2}$$

4.30

Case III: Outside the sphere (r>R)

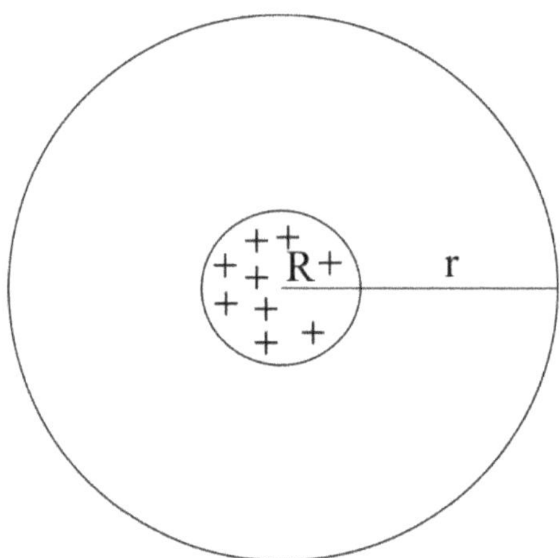

Fig 4.17 Field for a point outside the sphere

We will apply Gauss theorem in this too. This is the electric field outside the sphere.

If we plot these variations on a graph we will get the following graph below. Since this is a solid sphere, it has charge inside it as well and that is why the electric field is non zero. In case of a hollow spherical shell, the electric field inside the shell is zero.

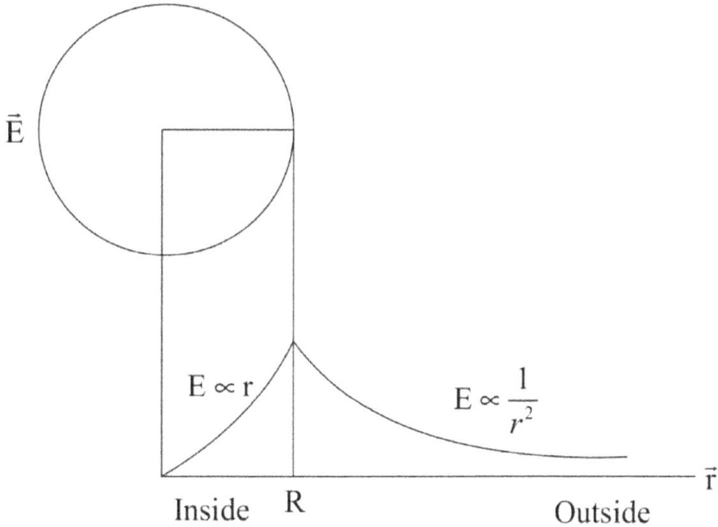

Fig 4.18 variation of electric field with distance

4.10 Potential difference and Potential

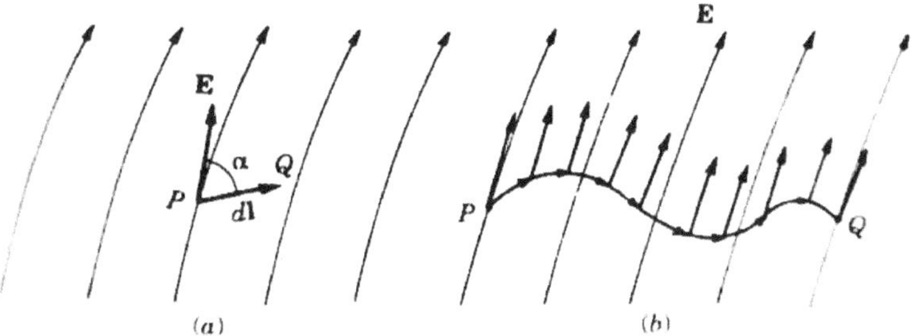

Fig 4.19 Movement of test charge in a electric field

In the gravitational field, when a mass moves from a higher elevation to a lower elevation, it loses some potential energy and vice versa. Likewise, in electric field, we can state that the test charge has certain potential energy associated with it by virtue of its location in the electric field. The work done, (W) as given by

$$W = -q \int_{P}^{Q} E.dl$$

4.31

W is the gain of potential energy associated with the movement of charge from P to Q. -ve sign in (3.4) will give potential rise, and if -ve sign is removed it will give fall of potential.

The potential difference V is defined as the work done (by an external source) in moving a unit positive charge from one point to another in an electric field

$$Potential\ difference = V = - \int_{initial}^{final} \overline{E}.\overline{dl}$$

4.32

As nomenclature, the potential difference between the two points A and B is written as V_{AB} and is the work done in moving the unit charge from B to A. Refer Fig. 4.20, in a uniform field the positive test charge is moved from point B to point A opposite to the field direction. Work has to he performed by external source in order to move a test charge from B to A against the field and the potential difference between point A and B is

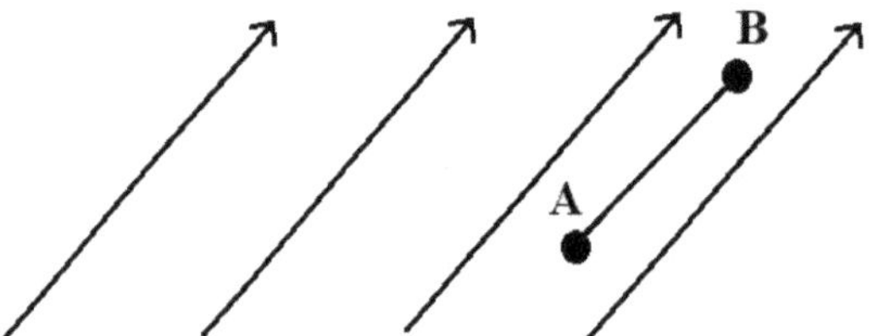

Fig. 4.20 Movement of a test charge from B to A for the concept of potential difference V_{AB}.

$$V_{AB} = -\int_{A}^{B} \overline{E}.\overline{dl}$$

4.33

The unit of potential difference is joule/coulomb or volt.

It is often convenient to speak of the potential, or absolute potential of a point, rather than the potential difference between two points, but this means only that we measure potential difference with respect to a reference point having zero potential. In actual case, the ground has zero potential; but for our case we shall assume a point at infinity to have zero potential. With this concept in mind we may write potential at point A as VA and potential at point B as V, then

$V_{AB} = V_A - V_B$ 4.34

Both V_A and V_B have same zero reference point.

The potential field of a point charge:

Let us consider the electric field due a point charge, Fig. 4.21, and two points A and B in the electric field situated at distances r, and r, respectively

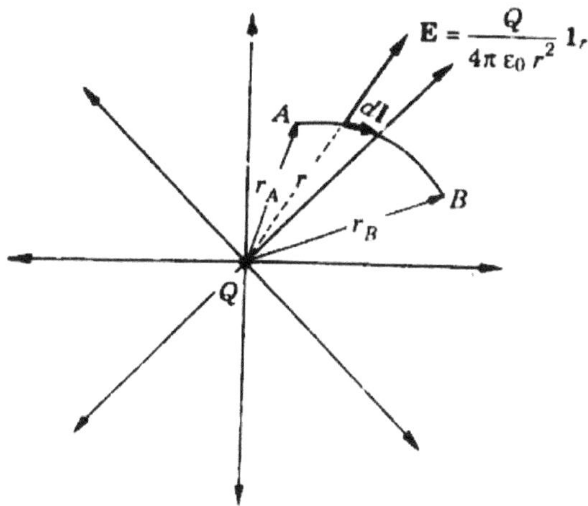

Fig 4.21 Computation of potential between two points in an electric field of a point charge

From the point charge. The field intensity at a distance r from a point charge is

$$\overline{E} = \frac{1}{4\pi\varepsilon_0} \times \frac{q}{r^2}\,\hat{n}$$

4.35

The potential difference between A and B can be computed for any specified path between A and B. Considering spherical coordinates the differential length vector is

$$d\bar{l} = dr\,\hat{n} + r\,d\theta\,n_\theta + r\sin\theta\,d\phi\,n_\phi$$

4.36

We have

$$V_{AB} = -\int_A^B \overline{E}.d\overline{l}$$

$$V_{AB} = -\int_{r=r_B}^{r=r_A} \left(\frac{1}{4\pi\varepsilon_0} \times \frac{q}{r^2}\hat{n} \right) \cdot \left(dr\,\hat{n} + r\,d\theta\, n_\theta + r\sin\theta\, d\phi\, n_\phi \right)$$

$$V_{AB} = \int_{r_A}^{r_B} \left(\frac{1}{4\pi\varepsilon_0} \times \frac{q}{r^2} \right) dr = \frac{q}{4\pi\varepsilon_0 r_A} - \frac{q}{4\pi\varepsilon_0 r_B}$$

4.37

It becomes clear from (4.37) that potential difference between two points is dependent only upon their distance from the point charge and not on the path from B to A. Since $V_{AB} = V_A - V_B$ we can write,

$$V_{AB} = \frac{q}{4\pi\varepsilon_0} \left(\frac{1}{r_A} - \frac{1}{r_B} \right)$$

4.38

$$\text{if } r_B \to \infty \text{ then}$$

$$V_{AB} = V_A = \frac{q}{4\pi\varepsilon_0 r_A}$$

4.39

This is called absolute potential at point A.

In general, for any point P, distance r from a point charge q the absolute potential is given by

$$V_r = \frac{q}{4\pi\varepsilon_0 r}$$

4.40

$$V_r = -\int_{\infty}^{r} \overline{E}.d\overline{l}$$

4.41

This is the work done per coulomb to bring a positive test charge from infinity to the point against the field.

4.11 Capacitance

It is the capability of an element to store electric charge within it. A capacitor stores electric energy in the form of electric field being established by the two polarities of charges on the two electrodes of a capacitor.

Quantitatively capacitance is a measure of charge per unit voltage that can be stored in an element. The unit of capacitance (C) is Farad (F). The capacitance is said to be one Farad provided one coulomb of charge can be stored with one volt across the two electrodes of the element. The element, which has capacitance, is called capacitor.

q being the amount of charge that can be stored in a capacitor of capacitance C against a potential difference of v volts, we can write

$$C = \frac{q}{v}$$

4.42

i.e,

$$i = C\frac{dv}{dt} \qquad \left[as\ i = \frac{dq}{dt}\right]$$

4.43

Where lower case letters represent the instantaneous values of the respective parameters;

$$dv = \frac{1}{C}i\,dt$$

$$\int_{v_1}^{v_2} dv = \frac{1}{C}\int_{0}^{t} i\,dt$$

$$4.44$$

v_0 = initial voltage of capacitor, v_t = final voltage of capacitor)

$$v_t - v_0 = \frac{1}{C} \int_0^t i\,dt$$

$$v_t = \frac{1}{C} \int_0^t i\,dt + v_0$$

$$4.45$$

The power absorbed by the capacitor is given by

$$P = vi = vC \frac{dv}{dt}$$

$$4.46$$

And the energy stored by the capacitor is

$$W = \int_0^t P\,dt = \int_0^t vC \frac{dv}{dt}\,dt = \frac{1}{2} Cv^2$$

$$4.47$$

Thus we observe that, the voltage across the capacitor being constant, current through it is zero. This means that the capacitor, on application of dc voltage and with no initial charge first acts as short circuit but as soon as the full charge it retains, the capacitor behaves an open circuit. Also, a capacitor never dissipates energy and only stores it. It can store finite amount energy, even if the current through it is zero.

Series and parallel connection of capacitances:

Let us assume a voltage v being applied in a circuit containing two capacitances C1 and C2 in series. Let C be their equivalent capacitance and i be the series current.

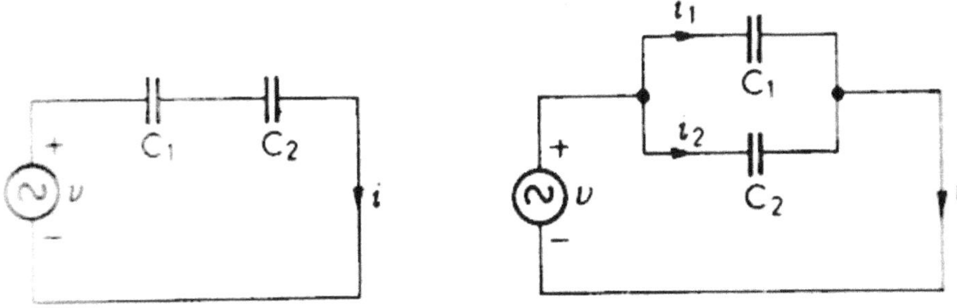

Fig. 4.22 Series connection and Parallel connection of capacitances

Here, the applied voltage in the summation of the individual voltage drops across C1 and C2.

$$v = drop\ across\ C_1 + drop\ across\ C_2$$

$$or\ \ \frac{1}{C}\int idt = \frac{1}{C_1}\int idt + \frac{1}{C_2}\int idt$$

$$\frac{1}{C} = \frac{1}{C_1} + \frac{1}{C_2}$$

$$i.e,\ C = \frac{C_1 C_2}{C_1 + C_2}$$

4.48

On the other hand, if the capacitances C1 and C2 are in parallel, i1 and i2 being the branch currents, the total current i is given by

$$i = i_1 + i_2$$

$$C\frac{dv}{dt} = C_1\frac{dv}{dt} + C_2\frac{dv}{dt}$$

$$i.e,\ C = C_1 + C_2$$

4.49

Capacitance of a parallel plate capacitor:

A Capacitor which can store 1 C of charge with a potential difference of 1 V has a capacitance of 1 F. Normally, the capacitance of a capacitor is written in micro farad ($1\mu F = 10^{-6}$ F) or pico farad 1 pF=10^{-12} F . The capacitance of a capacitor depends on the physical dimensions and the nature of insulating material (its permittivity), and is independent of the charge and voltage. An increase in applied voltage increases the charge stored, but the ratio of the charge to voltage remains constant.

A simple parallel plate capacitor consists of two parallel conducting plates of area A separated by à distance d, Fig. 4.23. We assume here that the medium between the plates is air or vacuum (permittivity = E). When a dielectric of permittivity, ε greater than air is used, the capacitance is increased.

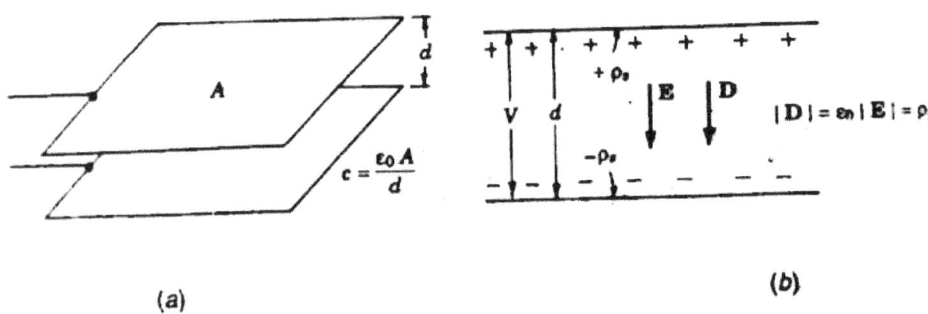

Fig 4.23 **parallel plate capacitor**

Assuming the charge density on the plates to be uniform, the total charge on the plate is

$Q = \rho_s A$ 4.50

Where ρ_s is surface charge density C/m².

Each plate, being a conductor is equipotential surface. Hence, the field between the parallel plates is simply

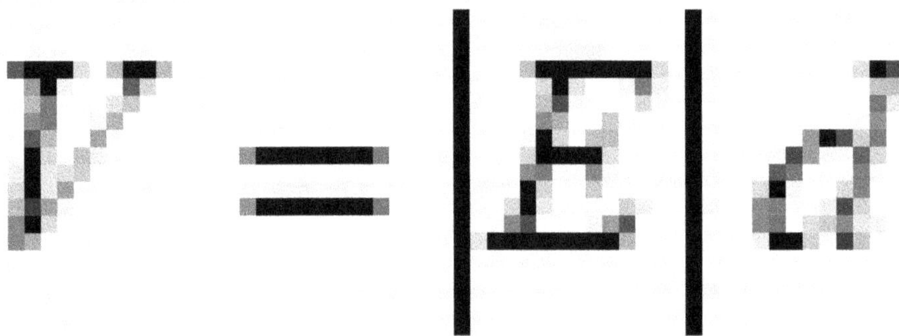

$$V = |E|d$$

4.51

The magnitude of the flux density D between the plates equals the surface charge density ρ_s

$$|D| = \rho_z = \varepsilon_0 |E| \quad C/m^2$$

4.52

The capacitance is then,

$$C = \frac{Q}{V} = \frac{\rho_z A}{Ed} = \frac{\varepsilon_0 E A}{Ed} = \frac{\varepsilon_0 A}{d}$$

4.53

Where ε_0= permittivity of air = 8.854 x 10-12 F/m, A is area of the plates, d is separation between the plates.

Dielectric and its effect on capacitance

Dielectric

Dielectrics are basically insulating and non-conducting substances. They are bad conductors of electric current. Dielectrics are capable of holding electrostatic charges while emitting minimal energy. This energy is usually in the form of heat. The materials that are very poor conductor of electric current but have the ability to store electric charges are called as dielectrics. The dielectric separates the metal plates of capacitor. A simple parallel plate capacitor, like two metal plates facing each other with air in between. When you charge it up, electrons pile up on one plate, creating a negative charge, while the other plate becomes positively charged. Some examples for dielectric materials, include ceramic, plastic, mica, glass etc.

How does the dielectric increase the capacitance of a capacitor?

The electric field between the plates of parallel plate capacitor is directly proportional to capacitance C of the capacitor. The strength of the electric field is reduced due to the presence of dielectric. If the total charge on the plates is kept constant, then the potential difference is reduced across the capacitor plates. In this way, dielectric increases the capacitance of the capacitor.

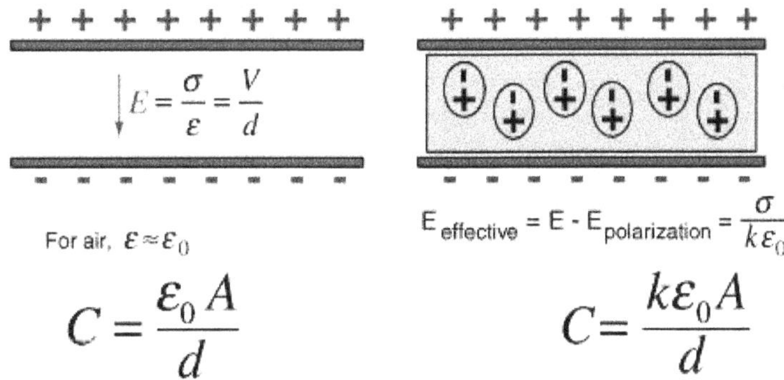

Fig 4.24 shows capacitance is increased by factor k

Application of Dielectrics in Capacitors

1. Capacitor Functionality: Dielectrics are widely used in capacitors to store energy in an electric field between plates.
2. Signal Filtering: They help filter out unwanted signal noise in resonant circuits.
3. Power Burst: Dielectrics can provide a quick burst of power to other components.
4. Desirable Features: High electrical resistivity and low dielectric loss are important characteristics because dielectrics primarily work as insulators rather than charge retainers.
5. Insulation: Dielectrics are commonly used for insulating wires, cables, and similar applications.
6. Sensor Technology: Dielectrics is also used in in sensor technology.

4.12 Dielectric Break Down

A dielectric material is ideally a perfect insulator. They are used in electrical and electronic circuits as insulators and as dielectric medium in capacitors. When a dielectric is subjected to an electric field, there is a limit to the field up to which it acts as a perfect insulator beyond a certain critical electric field, the dielectric starts to conduct, and it is said to have reached its breakdown electric field .the electric field at which the dielectric breaks down is called its dielectric strength and it is measured in Volts/m.

There are three breakdown mechanisms in a dielectric:

a. Avalanche break down
b. Thermal breakdown
c. Defect breakdown

a. Avalanche break down

This can be explained on the basis of band theory of insulators discussed in chapter dielectrics have completely filled valence band and a wide energy gap (>5eV) between the valence band, and the conduction band, when a dielectric is subjected to high electric fields the electrons in the valence band acquire sufficient energy to overcome the large energy gap and get excited to the conduction band. The mobile electrons get highly accelerated in the high electric field and so by collisions they excite more electrons to the conduction band .thus more and more electrons are released to the conduction band resulting in an avalanche of conduction electrons .ultimately the material becomes highly conducting and is said to have reached the breakdown field.

2. Thermal break down

When high frequency ac field is applied to a dielectric there will be energy loss ,as discussed earlier, and this energy has to be dissipated as heat energy .if the dissipations is not effective , due to poor thermal conductivity of the dielectric ,the material gets heated up and may cause melting of the dielectric .this is called thermal break down.

3. Defect breakdown

This type of break down occurs in dielectric materials in which there are defects like cracks and pores .gases can collect in the cracks and pores. At high electric field, local electric field at the small cracks and pores will be so high that gas discharge will occur ,causing breakdown of the dielectric.

4.13 Numerical Problem and Solutions

1. Three Capacitors 10, 20, 25 μF are connected in Parallel with a 250V Supply. Calculate the Equivalent Capacitance.

Solution-

$C1 = 10\mu F = 10 \times 10\text{-}6$ F, $C2 = 20\mu F = 20 \times 10\text{-}6$ F, $C3 = 25\mu F = 25 \times 10\text{-}6$ F

Equivalent capacitance of a parallel combination is,

$Cp = C1 + C2 + C3 = 10 + 20 + 25$

Cp = 55 μF (**Answer**).

2. Two Condensers of Capacities 10 μF and 25 μF are charged to 12 V and 24 V respectively. What is the Common Potential When they are connected in Parallel?

Solution-

C1 = 10 μF, C2 = 25 μF, V1 = 12 V, V2 = 24 V, V=?

Charge on 1st condenser,

Q1 = C1V1 = 10 × 10^{-6} × 12 = 120 × 10^{-6} C

Charge on 2nd condenser,

Q2 = C2V2 = 25 × 10^{-6} × 24 = 600 × 10^{-6} C

Total charge Q = Q1 + Q2 = 120 × 10^{-6} + 600 × 10^{-6}

Q = 720 × 10^{-6} C

Equivalent capacitance of a parallel combination is,

Cp = C1 + C2 = 10 + 25 = 35 μF

If V is common potential,

Q = CV

V= Q/C

Hence V= 720/35 = 20.57 V (**Answer**).

3. Determine the amount of charge stored on either plate of a capacitor (4x10^{-6} F) when connected across a 12 volt battery.

Solution-

C = Q/V

4x10^{-6} = Q/12

Q = 48x10^{-6} C (**Answer**).

4. A parallel plate capacitor is constructed of metal plates, each with an area of 0.2 m^2. The capacitance is 7.9nF. Determine the plate separation distance.

Solution-

C = εoA/d

7.9x10^{-9} = 8.85x10^{-12}(0.2)/d

d = 2.2x10^{-4} m = 0.22 mm (**Answer**).

5. C1 = 10 F and C2 = 5 F. Determine the effective capacitance for C1 and C2 connected in series and in parallel.

Solution-

In series:

1/C = 1/C1 + 1/C2

1/C = 1/10 + 1/5

C = 3.3 F (**Answer**).

In parallel:

C = C1 + C2

C = 10 + 5 = 15 F (**Answer**).

6. Find the equivalent capacitance of the combination shown in fig 4.25

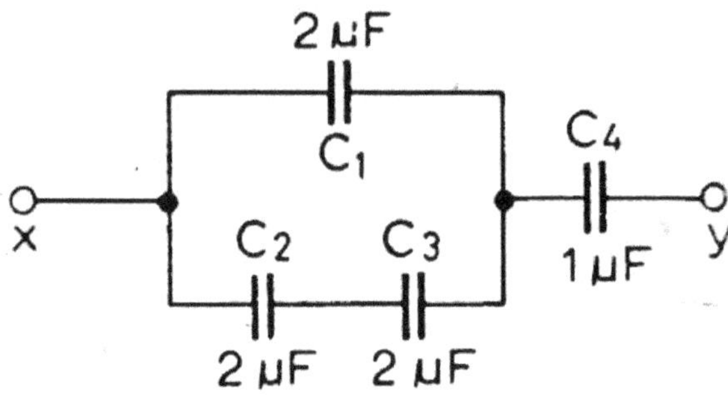

Fig 4.25 combination of capacitance

Solution-

Here C2 & C3 is in series and the combination of C2 and C3 are in parallel with C1 and this total combination is in series with C4.

Hence equivalent capacitance Ca for C2 & C3 is (2x2)/(2+2)=1μF.

How equivalent capacitance Cb for Ca & C1 is 1+2=3 μF.

Net equivalent capacitance for Cb & C4 is (3x1)/(3+1)=3/4μF **(Answer)**.

7. Evaluate the circuit shown in Fig 4.26 to determine the effective capacitance and then the charge and voltage across each capacitor.

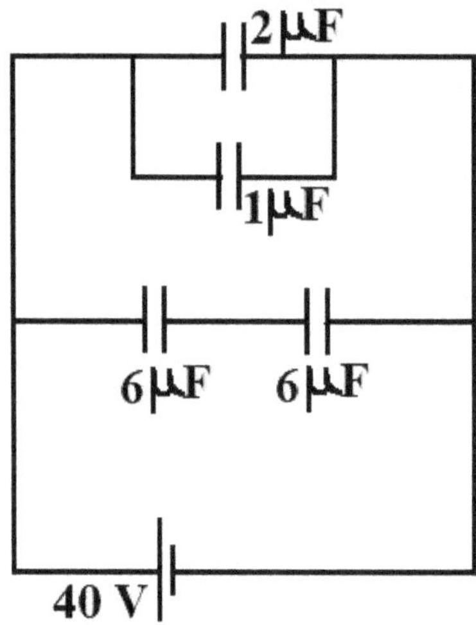

Fig 4.26 combination of capacitance

Solution-

The equivalent capacitance is 6 μF. The voltage across the equivalent capacitance is 40 v as is the voltage across the 3 μF capacitors and is the same as the 1 μF and 2 μF capacitors.

The charge on the 1 μF capacitor:

C = Q/V

1 μF = Q/40

Q = 40 μC

Then the charge on the 2 μF capacitor:

C = Q/V

2 μF = Q/40

Q = 80 μC

Again the charge on the 3 μF capacitors:

C = Q/V

3 μF = Q/40

Q = 120 μC

This is the same charge on each of the 6 μF capacitors.

Therefore the voltage on each of the 6 μF capacitors:

C = Q/V

6 μF = 120 μC/V

V = 20 v **(Answer).**

8. Evaluate the circuit shown in Fig 4.27 to determine the effective capacitance and then the charge and voltage across each capacitor.

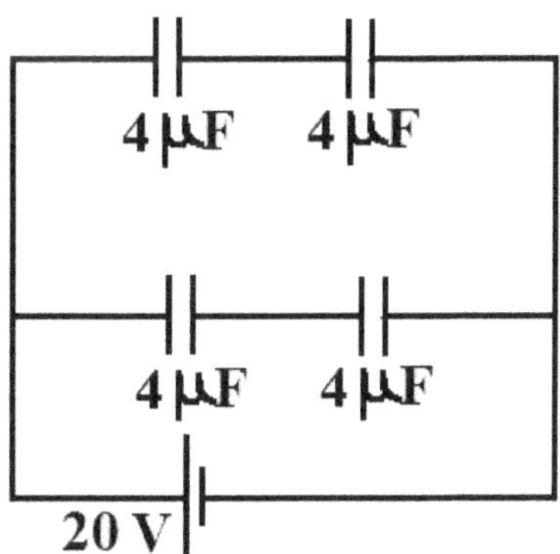

Fig 4.27 combination of capacitance

Solution-

The equivalent capacitance is 4 μF. The voltage across the equivalent capacitor is 20 volts.

This voltage is also across both of the 2 μF capacitors that were created by the series combinations in each branch.

Hence the charge on each 2 μF capacitor:

C = Q/V

2 μF = Q/20

Q = 40 μC

The 4 μF capacitors in each branch have the same charge as the 2 μF capacitors. Use this to find the voltage across each:

C = Q/V

4 μF = 40 μC/V

V = 10 volts **(Answer).**

Each of the original 4 μF capacitors have a charge of 40 μC and a voltage of 10 volts.

9. A dipole is set up with a charge magnitude of 2×10^{-7} C for each charge (one is positive and the other is negative.) The distance between the charges is 0.15 m. What are the magnitude and direction of the E-field at the midpoint of the dipole? (Assume the positive charge is on the left.) Also determine the force magnitude and direction for an electron at that position in the field.

Solution-

The E-field from both charges will point to the right, thus the overall E-field is to the right. The magnitude of the overall E-field is the addition of the two E-fields caused by the charges:

$E = E_+ + E_- = kq/r^2 + kq/r^2 = kq(1/r^2 + 1/r^2)$

$E = (9x10^9)(2x10^{-7})(1/(0.15/2)^2 + 1/(0.15/2)^2)$

$E = 640000$ N/C

The force on the electron is F=qE

$F = (1.6x10^{-19})x(640000) = 1x10^{-13}$N **(Answer).**

10. How many electrons are needed to form a charge of –2.00 nC?

Solution-

All charged objects in nature carry charges that are integral multiples of the basic quantity of charge, q_e, any charge Q: $Q = nq_e$

$| q_e | = 1.60×10^{-19}$ C.

$$N = \frac{Q}{q_e} = \frac{-2.0 \times 10^{-9}}{1.6 \times 10^{-19}} = 1.25 \times 10^{10}$$

(Answer)

4.14 Objective Type questions with solution:

1. Coulomb is the unit of which quantity?

    a) Field strength b) Charge c) Permittivity d) Force

    Answer: b

    2. Coulomb law is employed in

    a) Electrostatics b) Magnetostatics c) Electromagnetics d) Maxwell theory

    Answer: a

    3. Find the force between 2C and -1C separated by a distance 1m in air (in newton).

    a) $18 X 10^6$ b) $18 X 10^9$ c) $18 X 10^{-6}$ d) $18 X 10^8$

    Answer: b

    4. Two 1 Coulomb charges are kept at 1m distance in air medium. Force of attraction or repulsion between them will be _________

    a) $9x10^9$ N b) 1 dyne c) 1 N d) $3x10^3$ N

    Answer: a

    5. Let B be the midpoint of AC. Two point charges Q are placed at A and C. What should be the value of charge placed at B so that the system remains at equilibrium?

    a) –Q/2 b) –Q/4 c) +Q/2 d) +Q/4

    Answer: b

    6. If the force between two charges is 9N, what will be the force if the distance between them is doubled and both the charges are increased to √2 times?

    a) 9N b) 4.5N c) 3N d) 3.75N

    Answer: b

    7. Two charges q1, q2 exert some amount of force on each other. What will happen to the force on q1 if another charge q3 is brought close to them?

    a) The force will increase b) The force will decrease c) The force remains the same

    d) The force may increase or decrease depending on whether q3 is positive or negative

    Answer: d

8. Two negative charges are kept at a certain distance in the air medium. What will happen if a dielectric slab is inserted between them?

a) The slab will get heated b) Current will flow through the slab

c) Two charges will attract each other d) The net force between the charges will be reduced

Answer: d

9. What is the C.G.S. unit of charge?

a) Stat Coulomb b) Coulomb c) EMU d) Pascal

Answer: a

10. Coulomb's Law is valid for _______

a) Only point charge b) For both point charge and distributed charge

c) Only distributed charges d) Neither distributed nor point charge

Answer: a

11. The amount of force exerted on a unit positive charge in an electric field is known as ______

a) Electric field intensity b) Electric flux c) Electric potential d) Electric lines of force

Answer: a

12. The direction of electric field created by a negative charge is ____________

a) Directed outwards b) Directed towards the charge

c) Maybe outwards or towards the charge d) Circular in shape

Answer: b

13. Electric field inside a hollow conducting sphere _______

a) Increases with distance from the center of the sphere

b) Decreases with distance from the center of the sphere

c) Is zero

d) May increase or decrease with distance from the center

Answer: c

14. A uniformly charged sphere of radius R has charge +Q. A point charge $-q$ is placed at a distance of 2R from the center of the sphere. The point charge will execute the simple harmonic motion. The statement is ______

a) False b) True

Answer: a

15. Electric field is a ________

a) Scalar quantity b) Vector quantity c) Tensor quantity d) Quantity that has properties of both scalar and vector

Answer: b

16. V/m is the unit of _______

a) Electric field intensity b) Electric flux c) Electric potential d) Charge

Answer: a

17. Find the electric field intensity at 10cm away from a point charge of 100 esu.

a) 1 dyne/esu b) 10 dyne/esu c) 100 dyne/esu d) 9×10^9 dyne/esu

Answer: a

18. What is the dimensional formula of capacitance of a capacitor?

a) $M^1L^2T^{-4}I^{-2}$ b) $M^{-1}L^{-2}T^4I^2$ c) $M^{-1}L^{-2}T^6$ d) $M^{-2}L^2T^4$

Answer: b

19. What is the value of capacitance of a capacitor if it has a charge of 9C and voltage of 5V?

a) 1.8F b) 45F c) 4.5F d) 8.1F

Answer: a

20. The electric potential difference between two points is a path function. The statement is

a) True b) False

Answer: b

21. Earth's potential is ________

a) Zero b) Highly positive c) Highly negative d) Varies from place to place

Answer: a

22. Work done to bring a unit positive charge from infinity to a point in an electric field is known as

a) Electric potential b) Electric field intensity

c) Electric dipole moment d) The total energy of the point charge

Answer: a

23. What is the dimension of electric potential?

a) $[M\,L\,T^{-2}]$ b) $[M\,L\,T^{-3}I]$ c) $[M\,L\,T^{-3}I^{-1}]$ d) $[M\,L^2\,T^{-3}I]$

Answer: c

24. What happens to the capacitance when a dielectric material is inserted between the plates of a parallel plate capacitor?

a) Capacitance decreases b) Capacitance remains same

c) Capacitance increases d) Depends upon the material of the dielectric

Answer: c

25. How is the electric field between the two plates of a parallel plate capacitor?

a) Zero b) Uniform c) Maximum d) Minimum

Answer: b

26. Identify the factor on which the capacitance of a parallel plate capacitor does not depend.

a) Permeability of the medium between the plates b) Area of the plates

c) Distance between the plates d) The permittivity of the medium between the plates

Answer: a

27. What is the net electric field in the outer regions above the upper plate and below the lower plate in a parallel plate capacitor?

a) Maximum b) Uniform c) Zero d) Minimum

Answer: c

28. In the inner region between the two capacitor plates, the electric fields due to the two charged plates are zero.

a) True b) False

Answer: b

29. A parallel plate capacitor has a plate area of 100 cm^2 and is separated by a distance of 20 mm. Find its capacitance.

a) 6.425×10^{-12} F b) 5.425×10^{-12} F c) 4.425×10^{-12} F d) 3.425×10^{-12} F

Answer: c

30. How does the potential difference change with the effect of the dielectric when the battery is kept disconnected from the capacitor?

a) Increases b) Decreases c) Remains constant d) Becomes zero

Answer: b

4.15 Important Questions:

1. Why do the electrostatic field lines not form closed loop?
2. Why do the electric field lines never cross each other?
3. Why must electrostatic field at the surface of a charge every point? Give reason.
4. State Coulomb's law of Force. What are the limitations of Coulomb's law?
5. Derive the vector form of Coulomb Law of Force.
6. Two point charges q1 and q2 are placed at a distance d apart as shown in the figure. The electric field intensity is zero at the point P on the line joining them as shown. Write two conclusions that you can draw from this.
7. Define dipole moment of an electric dipole. Is it a scalar quantity or a vector quantity?

8. Draw a plot showing the variation of electric field (E) with distance r due to a point charge Q.
9. A proton is placed in a uniform electric field directed along the position X-axis. In which direction will it tend to move?
10. Two point charges having equal charges separated by lm distance experience a force of 8 N. What will be the force experienced by them if they are held in water at the same distance? (Given, Kwater = 80).
11. A metallic sphere is placed in a uniform electric field as shown in the figure. Which path is followed by electric field lines and why?
12. Two charges + Q and -Q are kept at points $(-x_2, 0)$ and $(x_t, 0)$ respectively, in the XY-plane. Find the magnitude and direction of the net electric field at the origin (0, 0).
13. If the radius of the Gaussian surface enclosing a charge is halved, how does the electric flux through the Gaussian surface change?
14. Two charged conducting spheres of radii r1 and r2 connected to each other by a wire. Find the ratio of electric fields at the surfaces of the two spheres.
15. Draw the shapes of the suitable Gaussian surfaces while applying Gauss' law to calculate the electric field due to

(i)a uniformly charged long straight wire.
(ii)a uniformly charged infinite plane sheet.

1. Using Gauss' law, obtain the expression for the electric field due to uniformly charged solid sphere of radius R and volume charge density ρ at a point outside, on the surface and inside the sphere.
2. Using Gauss' law, obtain the expression for the electric field due to uniformly charged spherical shell of radius R at a point outside the shell. Draw a graph showing the variation of electric field with r, for $r > R$ and $r < R$.
3. Can we have non-zero electric potential in space, where electric field strength is zero?
4. Derive the expression of equivalent capacitance for capacitors connected in series and parallel.
5. How does the dielectric increase the capacitance of a capacitor?
6. State the application of Dielectrics in Capacitors. Define dielectric breakdown.
7. Two tiny spheres carrying charges 1.5μC and 2.5μC are located 30 cm apart. Find the potential and electric field at the mid-point of the line joining the two charges.
8. 17. The plates of a parallel plate capacitor have an area of 90cm^2 each and are separated by 2.5mm. The capacitor is charged by connecting it to a 400V supply. How much electrostatic energy is stored by the capacitor?
9. Explain what would happen if in the capacitor given in Exercise 2.8, a 3mm thick mica sheet (of dielectric constant =6) were inserted between the plates, (a) While the voltage supply remained connected. (b) After the supply was disconnected.
10. A 12pF capacitor is connected to a 50V battery. How much electrostatic energy is stored in the capacitor?

SOME FUNDAMENTAL CONSTANTS

Constant	*Symbol*	*Computational Value*
Speed of light in vacuum	c	3×10^8 ms^{-1}
Planck's constant	h	6.63×10^{-34} J.s $= 4.14 \times 10^{-21}$ MeVs
Permeability constant (vacuum)	μ_o	$4\pi \times 10^{-7} = 1.26 \times 10^{-6}$ H.m^{-1}
Permittivity constant (of vacuum)	$\epsilon_0 = \dfrac{1}{\mu_0 c^2}$	8.85×10^{-12} F$/$m ; $\dfrac{1}{4\pi \epsilon_0} = 8.99 \times 10^9 \dfrac{m}{F}$
Gravitational constant	G_1	6.67×10^{-11} Nm$^2/$kg^2
Boltzmann constant	k	1.38×10^{-23} J/K $= 8.62 \times 10^{-5}$ eV/K
Stefan-Boltzmann constant	$\sigma = \dfrac{\pi^2 k^2}{60 h^3 c^2}$	5.67×10^{-8} Wm^{-2}K^{-4}
Rydberg constant	$R = \dfrac{e^4 m_e}{8 h^3 \epsilon_0 c}$	1.10×10^7 m^{-1}
Faraday constant	$F_1 = N_A e$	9.65×10^4 C mol^{-1}
Avogadro number / constant	N_A	6.02×10^{23} mol^{-1}
Fine structure constant	$\sigma = \dfrac{e^2}{2 \epsilon_0 hc}$	$1/137$
Electron charge	$-e$	-1.6×10^{-19} c
Electron charge-to-mass ratio	$|e/m_e|$	1.76×10^{11} C kg^{-1}
Proton-electron mass ratio	m_p/m_e	1837
Electron Compton wavelength	λ_e	2.43×10^{12} m
Bohr radius	$a_0 = h^2/m_e e^2$	5.29×10^{-11} m $= 0.53$ Å
Bohr magneton	$|\mu_B| = eh/2m_e$	9.28×10^{-24} JT^{-1}

Anex Fig 1.0

Constant	Symbol	Computational Value
Magnetic flux quantum	$\Phi_0 = h/2e$	2.07×10^{-15} T.m^2
Quantized Hall resistance	R_H	$25800\ \Omega$
Electron magnetic moment	$\mu_e = -(1.001e\hbar)/2m_e$	-9.28×10^{-24} JT^{-1}
Proton magnetic moment	$\mu_P = 2.79e\hbar 2m_P$	1.41×10^{-26} JT^{-1}
Neutron magnetic moment	$\mu_n = 1.91e\hbar/2m_P$	-9.66×10^{-27} JT^{-1}
Electron rest mass	$m_p = 9.11 \times 10^{-31}$ kg	5.49×10^{-4} u $= 0.511$ MeV/C^2
Proton rest mass	$m_p = 1.673 \times 10^{-27}$ kg	$= 1.007$ u $= 938.3$ MeV / C^2
Neutron rest mass	$m_n = 1.675 \times 10^{-27}$ kg	$= 1.009$ u $= 939.6$ MeV / C^2
Alpha rest mass	$m_a = 6.65 \times 10^{-27}$ kg	$= 4.003$u $= 3728$ MeV / C^2

Anex Fig 2.0

www.ingramcontent.com/pod-product-compliance
Lightning Source LLC
Chambersburg PA
CBHW040145110726
48005CB00018B/2652